Contents

Acknowledgements

The author owes a debt to the many sources sifted through for this compilation. Although the primary sources were various foreign dictionaries, the following sources were especially useful and are commended:

Dictionary of Foreign Phrases and Classical Quotations ed. H.P. Jones (John Grant); *Dictionary of Foreign Terms and Phrases* by C.O.S. Mawson, ed. Eugene Ehrlich (Penguin); *A Dictionary of Foreign Words and Phrases in Current English* by Alan Bliss (Routledge); *Foreign Expressions* by B.A. Pythian (Headway: Hodder and Stoughton); *Concise Dictionary of 26 Languages* by Peter M. Bergman (Signet); *French False Friends* by C.W.E. Kirk-Greene (Routledge & Kegan Paul).

On idiomatic usage, Cassell's series on colloquial French, German, Italian and Spanish proved to be excellent reference books and are easily the best in this field. Harrap's *Harrap's English-French Slang Dictionary* and Genevieve's idiosyncratic *Merde!* (HarperCollins/Fontana) were trawled for some rude bits, while a few samplings from Henry Beard's *Latin for All Occasions* (Angus & Robertson) bring a dead language to life in a most engaging way.

Also consulted were Hugo's *Simplified System Phrase Books* (Hugo's Language Books Limited); Collins' phrase books and dictionaries (HarperCollins); Barron's Educational Series and *Instant* Foreign Language Programs for Travelers; and Berlitz's phrase books and dictionaries (Berlitz Publishing Co Ltd).

Graham King (1930-1999)

Graham King was born in Adelaide on October 16, 1930. He trained as a cartographer and draughtsman before joining Rupert Murdoch's burgeoning media empire in the 1960s, where he became one of Murdoch's leading marketing figures during the hard-fought Australian newspaper circulation wars of that decade. Graham King moved to London in 1969, where his marketing strategy transformed the *Sun* newspaper into the United Kingdom's bestselling tabloid; subsequently, after 1986, he successfully promoted the reconstruction of *The Sunday Times* as a large multi-section newspaper.

A poet, watercolourist, landscape gardener and book collector, Graham King also wrote a biography of Zola, *Garden of Zola* (1978) and several thrillers such as *Killtest* (1978). Other works include the novel *The Pandora Valley* (1973), a semi-autobiographical account of the hardships endured by the Australian unemployed and their families set in the 1930s.

In the early 1990s, inspired by the unreadability and impracticality of many of the guides to English usage in bookshops, Graham King developed the concept of a series of reference guides called The One-Hour Wordpower series: accessible, friendly guides designed to guide the reader through the maze of English usage. He later expanded and revised the texts to create an innovative series of English usage guides that would break new ground in their accessibility and usefulness. The new range of reference books became the Collins Wordpower series (see page 179), the first four titles being published in March 2000, the second four in May 2000. Graham King died in May 1999, shortly after completing the Collins Wordpower series.

Introduction

The great grammarian H.W. Fowler didn't mince his words on the practice of using foreign terms and expressions designed to go over the heads of the average English reader. 'To use French words,' he wrote, 'that your reader or hearer does not know or does not fully understand . . . is inconsiderate and rude. Display of superior knowledge is as great a vulgarity as display of superior wealth.'

Nevertheless, this infusion of foreign expressions into our reading, in newspapers, magazines and books, is a fact of life whether we like it or not. We have the choice, when encountering yet another burst of italics, of groaning and fetching the dictionary, with an excellent chance of searching in vain for the word or phrase, or blithely leaping over the intrusion and reading on, saddled with guilt and ignorance.

Perhaps we should remind ourselves that English, in any case, is a language that over the centuries has picked up words as a magnet picks up iron filings, so nothing has really changed. Take *Schadenfreude*, a German word meaning 'taking malicious pleasure from another's misfortune'. A decade or so ago you'd rarely have seen this word in print; now it's everywhere. In fact it is now considered to be naturalised into the language, it often loses its German capital 'S', it is featured in most English dictionaries, and fewer writers bother to italicise it any more.

That process has been repeated with tens of thousands of words, terms and sayings from other languages. Many of them are now so embedded in English that we simply couldn't do without them. Examples include *tête-à-tête, vis-à-vis, bête noire* and *bon mot*

1

from the French; *ad hoc*, 'et cetera' and *post mortem* from Latin; 'leitmotiv', *gesundheit* and 'wunderkind' from German; 'ombudsman' from Swedish, not to mention several hundred musical and operatic terms from Italian.

Perhaps this cherry-picking is a reflection of our ineptitude with other languages, for we are, among Europeans, at the bottom of the linguistic league, only a whisker ahead of Ireland. The proportion of Britons able to speak a foreign language is the lowest in the EU, where almost 100% of young people in Luxembourg, Denmark and Holland can speak a second language, most often English.

This book is not going to rectify the situation, but it may help us when we encounter a foreign word or saying which we do not understand. Indeed, it may even encourage some of us to use, with confidence, the odd *mot juste* in letters or reports or in our everyday speech.

No compilation of this kind can ever claim to include every foreign word, phrase or quotation waiting to trip us up. With some 6000 languages in the world, and with many of them containing thousands of words that might express a thought more aptly or colourfully or economically than our home-grown variety, such a collection is impossible to imagine.

But here, at least, is a concise selection that should prove useful to the contemporary reader and writer. It excludes many foreign words that now reside in any good comprehensive dictionary. It also excludes specialist terms, including those connected with music and opera; these will be found in most English dictionaries. On the other hand it includes a good many colloquial and even vulgar expressions not to be found in dictionaries but which are common enough in speech and print. The rationale behind this book is relevance to contemporary needs.

In the spirit of the *Wordpower* series of books on English usage and effective communication, the tone here is light, even light-hearted, and leavened throughout with intriguing and humorous observations on the world's languages and how we exploit them.

A Note on Pronunciation

The English or Continental pronunciation of Roman spelling has been used to convey, as far as possible, the sounds of words belonging to languages with non-Latin alphabets: Russian, Greek, Hebrew, Arabic, Japanese and Chinese (Pinyin).

Words and phrases which are often used orally amidst the English language (*après-ski, fruits de mer, nisi, repêchage* etc.) are accompanied by an indication of their pronunciation. As this guide is intended for English speakers, pronunciation is indicated by simple letter combinations like STY, HAY, GO, BOO and AK:

adieu	ah-DYUR
ex gratia	eks GRAH-shuh
mêlée	MEH-lay
sine die	see-nay DEE-ay

There are some traps. Words ending in '**-y**' may be pronounced differently:

early	UR-lee	(the 'long e' sound)
layby	LAY-bye	(the 'long i' sound)

To make the difference clear, the 'long e' sound is indicated by 'ee' to rhyme with **glee**, and the 'long i' sound by a 'y' to rhyme with **eye**.

A stressed syllable is capitalised:
kaffeeklatsch   KAF-ay-klatsh

Perhaps the biggest problem facing English speakers is
French nasalisation. 'Nasalisation' is required to pronounce
correctly words such as *vin* and *blanc de blancs*. Most people manage
to produce a sound like 'vang' for the former, which isn't too far
off the mark, and 'blonk duh blonk' for the latter, which all but
pedants find acceptable. But if you wish to do better you could try
to nasalise the relevant vowels, and to indicate this we have used
the following device:

blanc de blancs   blah(n) duh blah(n)
en passant   ah(n) PAS-sah(n)
coquilles St Jacques   koh-kee sah(n) zhahk

The (n) indicates that the preceding vowel sounds should
be followed by an 'ng' sound that somehow gets lost up the nose.
If you listen to a fluent French speaker, or to a language tape, you
should get the idea fairly quickly.

Guide to Abbreviations

Abor	Australian Aborigine
Arab	Arabic
Ch	Chinese
Dut	Dutch
Fr	French
Gael	Gaelic
Ger	German
Gk	Greek
Haw	Hawaiian
Heb	Hebrew
Hind	Hindustani
Hun	Hungarian
Ir	Irish
It	Italian
Jap	Japanese
Lat	Latin
Mao	Maori
Pers	Persian
Port	Portuguese
Rus	Russian
Sans	Sanskrit
Scand	Scandinavian
Scot	Scottish
Sp	Spanish

Swa	Swahili
Swed	Swedish
Turk	Turkish
Yidd	Yiddish

A

à bas [Fr] Down with.

abat-jour [Fr] Skylight; lampshade; an arrangement for
   reflecting light into a room.

à bientôt [Fr] (ah byah(n)-toh) Goodbye – see you again soon.

abonnement [Fr] A subscription; season ticket.

abseil [Ger] (AB-seyl) Descending a steep or vertical
   surface using a double rope which is recovered by the
   last climber down.

absit omen! [Lat] Touch wood!

a cappella [It] Unaccompanied choral music, literally
chapel style.

Accents make a difference

Would you wipe your sweating pâté? Spread your pate on a
crusty roll? That demonstrates the seriousness of accents –
marks indicating a special pronunciation and usually,
therefore, a special meaning. English doesn't possess any so
we're not as *au fait* with them as perhaps we should be.
Foreign languages, however, make up for that and to make
anything of them we should at least know the roles of the
most common accents and marks.

There's a view that, when foreign words are
'naturalised' into English their accents are customarily
dropped. But when is a word naturalised? The French word

café is seen more without its accent (which tells us what it is and how it should be pronounced: kaf-FAY) than with, but is this sensible? Perhaps it's fashionable for wideboys and Eastenders to pronounce it KAYF, but it is nevertheless glaringly wrong. The same applies to words such as *cliché, façade, mêlée, protégé* and hundreds of others; even in English the accents still provide a valuable guide to their correct pronunciation.

ACCENTS MAKE A DIFFERENCE

Accents also supply an even more vital steer to clarity and meaning. Peter, for example, is a common English forename offending nobody. But cross the Channel and add an accent – *péter* – and you have the French word meaning farting. There was an actual incident when the Royal Family forced Princess Margaret to abandon her love affair with the divorced Commander Peter Townsend. This was duly reported in the French newspapers but one mischievous scandal sheet headlined the event: PRINCESS MARGARET RENONCE A PETER – or, PRINCESS MARGARET GIVES UP FARTING.

Foreign languages based on the Latin alphabet often have fewer characters than the English alphabet but more than make up the difference with a multitude of accented vowels, marks and diphthongs. In German, all nouns and words used as nouns are capitalised. French is fly-specked with a range of accents. Spanish has inverted question and exclamation marks. Spanish and Portuguese have the sweet little tilde. To help you understand the roles of pronunciation marks here are those that you will encounter on your voyages through the major foreign languages:

Acute accent [´] Usually indicates a rise in the voice or some other quality.

Breve [˘] Indicates a short vowel

Cedilla [̧] Placed under a *c*, before *a*, *o*, or *u*, to indicate it should be pronounced with a soft c, not as a hard k.

Circumflex [^] Usually indicates the vowel should be pronounced with a rising or falling pitch.

Diaeresis [¨] Placed over the second of two adjoining vowels (eg naïve, Noël) to indicate that they should be pronounced separately.

Grave accent [`] Usually indicates a fall in the voice, or to be pronounced with a certain quality.

Háček [č] Czechoslovakian mark to indicate, for example, *Dvořák* is pronounced DVOR-zhak and not DVOR-rak.

Macron [¯] Indicates a long vowel sound.

Stød [ø] In Scandinavian languages indicates an

unwritten sound or glottal stop.

Tilde [~] Indicates a nasal sound achieved by touching the tongue against the palate, as in the Spanish *señor*.

Umlaut [¨] Warning that the marked vowel is affected by the preceding or following syllables.

accouchement [Fr] (ah-koosh-mah(n)) Period of confinement for childbirth.

acedia [Lat from Gk] Spiritual apathy and indifference. Has been anglicised to *accidie*.

acushla [Ir] (ah-koosh-luh) Darling; term of endearment. The term *macushla* (my pulse, my heartbeat) is an anglicism.

Adeste fideles [Lat] (ad-EST-tay fih-DAY-lees) First line of the hymn known in English as 'O come all ye faithful'.

à deux [Fr] (ah-DUR) For two; a meal for two; a meeting for two people.

ad hoc [Lat] For a particular purpose only; something hastily arranged.

ad hominem [Lat] Relating to a certain person; in an argument, appealing to the prejudices or emotions of the listener rather than to reason.

adieu [Fr] (ah-DYUR) Farewell.

ad infinitum [Lat] To infinity; without end.

ad interim [Lat] For the meantime; meanwhile.

adiós [Sp] Farewell.

ad libitum; ad lib [Lat] At a speaker's discretion; to improvise and speak or perform without preparation.

ad majorem Dei gloriam [Lat] For the greater glory of God. Motto of the Jesuits.

ad nauseam [Lat] To a sickening degree.

affaire [Fr] Affair; scandal.

affaire d'amour [Fr] Love affair.

affaire de cœur [Fr] Love affair; affair of the heart.

affaire d'honneur [Fr] (uh-FAYR doh-NUR) A matter of honour.

affiche [Fr] A poster; pasted wall notice or advertisement.

aficionado [Sp] (ah-fees-yuh-NAR-doh) An ardent enthusiast; in Spain, of bullfighting.

à fond [Fr] Thoroughly; to the end; to the bottom.

a fortiori [Lat] All the more; for similar but sounder reasons.

agent provocateur [Fr] (ah-zhah(n) prov-ok-uh-TUR) Someone who provokes another to commit a crime to provide evidence for a conviction.

agunot [Heb] In Orthodox Jewry, legally divorced women who cannot get a religious divorce and who wish to remain in the faith are called *agunot*, or 'chained women'. If they remarry in a Reform or Liberal synagogue their children are called *mamzerin*, or illegitimates.

à gogo [Fr] In abundance; galore.

agrégation [Fr] (ag-ray-GAS-yor(n)) The *concours d'agrégation* is the French competitive examination for teaching posts.

à huis clos [Fr] In private; in secret.

adeo in teneris consuescere multum est [Lat] 'As the twig is bent the tree inclines' – from Virgil.

aide-de-camp [Fr] (ay-duh-KAH(N)) Personal assistant to a senior military officer.

aide-mémoire [Fr] Notes to help the memory.

aîné [Fr] (ay-nay) Elder; always preceded by a name.

aïoli [Fr] A widely used garlic and oil sauce.

akvavit [Scand] See *aquavit*.

à la [Fr] In the manner of.

à la carte [Fr] Dishes chosen individually from the bill of fare, rather than as part of a set menu.

à la mode [Fr] Fashionable.

à l'anglaise [Fr] In the English style.

à la recherche du temps perdu [Fr] Literally 'in quest of
the past', Marcel Proust's seven-part novel usually
known in English as *Remembrance of Things Past*.

al dente [It] (al-DEN-tay) Cooked to retain firmness
(usually pasta); not too soft.

al fresco; alfresco [It] In the open air.

aliyah [Heb] Emigration to Israel.

allée [Fr] An avenue or path; usually through trees or
shrubs.

allemansrätten [Swed] A Swedish citizen's right to enter
private land.

*Alles was geschieht, vom Grössten bis zum Kleinsten,
geschieht notwendig* [Ger] Everything that happens,
from the greatest to the least, happens of necessity –
Schopenhauer's philosophy of life.

Alles zu seiner Zeit [Ger] Everything in its proper time.

allumeuse [Fr] A flirt; a woman who wilfully inflames
male passions only to deny them satisfaction.

alma mater [Lat] 'Bounteous mother'. Chummy title given
to ex-student's former school, college or university.

All-purpose letter in Latin

Despite their musty image there *are* Latin scholars with a
keen sense of humour. One of them is New Yorker Henry
Beard, who offers this letter in Latin to those who wish to
bemuse, confuse or delay:

Dominus meus,
Epistulam tuam accepi et rei cuius mentionem ibi
fecisti animadversionam mean promptissimam
plenissimamque dabo.
Semper vale et salve,

Which means:

Dear Sir,
I have received your letter and I will give the
matter to which you referred my promptest and
fullest attention.
Best wishes,

---

aloha [Haw] Hawaiian for hello and goodbye.

à l'outrance; à outrance [Fr] (ah-loo-TRAH(N)S) To the
bitter end; to the death.

alter ego [Lat] A very close and intimate friend; a person's
'second self'.

Alte Wunden bluten leicht [Ger] Old wounds quickly
bleed anew.

alumnus; pl. *alumni* [Lat] Former pupil or graduate of a
school or university.

amah [Port] (AH-mah) Strictly speaking, a wet-nurse, but
now generally used in the East to mean a maid, servant
or children's nurse.

amende honorable [Fr] A public apology for an insult.

amie [Fr] A mistress.

amorino [It] A cupid statue.

amor mío; mis amores [Sp] My love; my darling.

amor patriae [Lat] Patriotism; love of one's country.

amour [Fr] (ah-MOOR) A secret love affair.

amour de voyage [Fr] A cruise or shipboard romance.

amourette [Fr] A trivial love affair.

amour-propre [Fr] (ah-MOOR PROP-ruh) Self-respect,
self-esteem; inclined to vanity.

amuse-gueule [Fr] An appetizer served before a meal.

ancien régime [Fr] An old regime; specifically, the
government of France before the Revolution.

Anglee-ya [Rus] England.

Anglia [Lat] England.

angst [Ger] Acute feelings of anxiety, fear and remorse,
usually for no accountable reason.

anguis in herba [Lat] A snake in the grass.

angulus terrarum [Lat] A special or favourite corner of the earth.

animateur [Fr] Someone able to present complex and abstruse concepts in clear and accessible ways.

an-neel [Arab] The Nile.

Anno Domini [Lat] In the year of our Lord; in the Christian era. The date is usually preceded by the abbreviation AD.

anno regni [Lat] In the year of the reign.

annus horribilis [Lat] Awful year; used by Queen Elizabeth II to describe nosediving Royal Family fortunes in 1992.

annus mirabilis [Lat] Remarkable, wonderful year.

Anschauung [Ger] A philosophical intuition or insight.

Anschluss [Ger] A political and economic union; specifically the annexation of Austria by Nazi Germany in 1938.

ante bellum; antebellum [Lat] The period before a war; used widely to refer to the period before the American Civil War.

ante meridiem [Lat] Before noon. Abbreviated to a.m.

antipodes [Gk] Those parts of the globe opposite our own; a term widely applied to Australasia.

apartheid [Afrikaans] (a-PART-ayt) Former South African policy of racial segregation.

aperçu [Fr] (ap-er-SOO) An insight; an intuitive understanding.

apéritif [Fr] Alcoholic drink, often fortified wine, taken before a meal.

apocrypha [Lat] Writings or documents of doubtful authenticity or authorship.

apologia [Lat] A written defence of a person's (usually one's own) opinions.

Apologia pro vita sua [Lat] Cardinal Newman's 1864 account of his spiritual journey, now used to describe any significant autobiography.

a posteriori [Lat] Logical reasoning from facts and effects to cause; a principle requiring factual evidence to validate it.

apparat [Rus] Communist bureaucracy in the former USSR; its members and agents were **apparatchiks**.

appeler un chat un chat [Fr] Call a cat a cat.

appliqué [Fr] (ap-PLEE-kay) Designs made by stitching one material upon another.

après moi, le déluge [Fr] The usual English version, but the correct phrase is **après nous, le déluge,** meaning after us, the deluge; when we're gone let the heavens fall. In other words, nothing now is likely to survive for much longer.

après-ski [Fr] (ap-ray-skee) Socialising after a day's skiing.

a priori [Lat] Deductive reasoning from cause to effect, which without supporting observation leads to a conclusion. Such reasoning can, of course, lead to wrong conclusions.

apropos; apropos [Lat] (ap-pruh-POH) Pertinent; with regard to; appropriate.

aquavit; akvavit [Scand] Flavoured grain or potato-based spirit.

arabesque [Fr] In music and art, a form of complex decoration; a ballet pose.

arak; arrack [Arab] A coarse spirit distilled from rice, palm-tree sap and sugar.

arcanum, pl. **arcana** [Lat] Hidden secrets; deeply mysterious.

à rebours [Fr] Perversely; against the grain.

arête [Fr] Sharp mountain ridge formed by erosion.

argot [Fr] (AH-goh) Originally thieves' cant, now generally used to describe the insider jargon of any class or group.

arrivederci [It] Farewell (until we meet again).

arma virumque cano [Lat] Of arms and the man I sing

(Virgil).

armoire [Fr] A tall cupboard or wardrobe.

arrière-pensée [Fr] (ari-ayr-pah(n)-say) An unrevealed or reserved thought; an ulterior motive.

arriviste [Fr] (ar-rih-VEEST) Someone dedicated to ambition and determined to succeed; self-seeking.

arrondissement [Fr] (ah-roh(n)-DEES-mah(n)) Administrative subdivision of a *département* in France; subdivision of Paris.

arroyo [Sp] A steep gully or watercourse.

ars gratia artis [Lat] Art for art's sake.

ars longa, vita brevis [Lat] Art is long, life is short.

ashram [Sans] A religious retreat; a group that shares religious or social ideals.

assiette [Fr] A plate or platter of prepared food.

à tâtons [Fr] Tentative; groping; feeling your way.

atelier [Fr] Studio; workshop, especially of an artist or craftsman.

à tort et à travers [Fr] Haphazardly; confused.

à trois [Fr] (ah-TRWAH) For three; a meal for three; a meeting between three.

attaccabottoni [It] A 'buttonholer'; a bore.

attentisme [Fr] The philosophy of 'wait and see'.

auberge [Fr] A French inn.

auch das Schöne muss sterben [Ger] Even the beautiful must die (Schiller).

au contraire [Fr] (oh-koh(n)-trare) On the contrary.

au courant [Fr] (oh-koo-rah(n)) Up-to-date on current affairs.

au fait [Fr] (oh-FAY) Fully informed.

au fond [Fr] Fundamentally; basically; essentially.

auf Wiedersehen [Ger] (ow-FVEE-duh-zayn) Goodbye; until we meet again.

au grand sérieux [Fr] In all seriousness.

au grand galop [Fr] At full gallop; at full tilt.

au gratin [Fr] (oh-grah-ta(n)) Food covered and baked with breadcrumbs and sometimes grated cheese.

auguste [Fr] A circus clown.

auld lang syne [Scot] Old times; times past.

au mieux [Fr] At best.

au naturel [Fr] (oh-natch-yoo-REL) Natural; naked.

au pair [Fr] (oh-PAIR) Commonly used in Britain to describe young people from other countries who help with housework and childcare in exchange for board and pocket money.

au pied de la lettre [Fr] Literally, to the last detail. Often abbreviated to *au pied*.

au poivre [Fr] Cooked with pepper.

au revoir [Fr] (oh-ruh-VWAHR) Goodbye; until we meet again.

aurora australis [Lat] The southern lights of the Antarctic regions.

aurora borealis [Lat] The northern lights of the Arctic regions.

aus den Augen, aus dem Sinn [Gen] Out of sight, out of mind.

au sérieux [Fr] Seriously; earnestly.

Auslander [Ger] To Germans, an outsider or foreigner.

Australian and Strine

Australian as a foreign language? Not quite. Although faced with a plethora of outback imagery ('I'm flat out like a lizard drinkin'), urban crudity ('park a tiger', 'cry Ruth', 'technicolour yawn' and 300 other synonyms for vomiting) and colourful slang ('I'm as dry as a dead dingo's donger') we still manage to grasp antipodean meanings without the need for translation.

But the same can't be said for **Strine,** the very marrow of Australian speech, delivered primarily through the nose and partly through a slot formed by the mouth narrow enough not to let flies in. **Strine** (Australyin – Austrine – Strine) has its own rules too – radical abbreviation. Thus a 'bottle of wine' reduces to 'bolla wine'; 'Have you eaten yet?' becomes 'Jeetyet?' and a 'couple of minutes' is reduced to 'garbler mince'. Here's a small selection of translations:

egg nisher	air conditioner
baked necks	bacon and eggs
Gunga Din, door's locked	Can't get in, the door's locked
gest vonner	guest of honour
num butter buncha drongos	nothing but a bunch of drongos
top hip ride	top of the hit parade
gissa lookcha	give us a look at you
check etcher check yet?	did you get your cheque yet?

auteur [Fr] A film director who so powerfully influences a film (departing from the original story, script or source) that he is considered its author.

autobahn [Ger] German motorway.

auto-da-fé [Port]; *auto-de-fé* [Sp] A public burning (formerly people, now books and objects such as flags).

autoestrada [Port] Portuguese motorway.

autopista [Sp] Spanish motorway.

autoroute [Fr] French motorway.

autostrada [It] Italian motorway.

autres temps, autres mœurs [Fr] (oh-truh-TAH(N), oh-truh-MUHRS) Other times, other ways; customs change with the times.

avant-courier [Fr] A precursor; a forerunner.

avant-garde [Fr] (av-var(n)-GARD) Pioneering, especially in the arts; innovative; experimental.

avant la lettre [Fr] Before a word was created to define an event, object, etc.

avatar [Sans] The earthly incarnation of a deity; the manifestation of an idea or principle in concrete or bodily form.

ave atque vale [Lat] Hail and farewell!

Ave Maria [Lat] Hail Mary! The angelic greeting to the Virgin; the prayer that begins with these words; the bell summoning the faithful to devotion.

avoirdupois [Fr] From *aver de peis* (goods of weight), the system of weights (tons, hundredweights, pounds and ounces) still used in some English-speaking countries.

avoir les cuisses légères [Fr] Literally, 'to possess light thighs'; colloquial expression for a woman of easy virtue.

a vuestra salud [Sp] Your good health.

ayah [Port] A maid, nursemaid or governess, usually to Europeans in Africa and the East.

ayatollah [Pers] An Iranian Shiite religious leader.

ayurveda [Sans] Ancient Indian medical system for healing and prolonging life.

azan [Arab] The five-times-daily Muslim call to prayer by a muezzin from a minaret.

azotea [Sp] A flat roof used as a terrace for living and entertaining.

B

baas [Dut] Boss or employer, in some African countries.

babu [Hind] Literally 'father', now an Indian official or clerk who writes in English.

babushka [Rus] A grandmother; also a headscarf worn by peasant women.

baccalauréat [Fr] French pre-university school-leaving examination.

bagarre [Fr] A scuffle; brawl.

bagno [It] Originally a prison or slave-house; brothel; bath-house.

baguette [Fr] The long French bread stick.

baignoire [Fr] A theatre box at stalls level.

bain-marie [Fr] Large pan of boiling water into which saucepans are placed for simmering food or keeping it hot.

Don't make a boner with *baiser*!

The meaning of *baiser* in some French-English dictionaries is still shown as **to kiss**, which is its correct original definition. If a scholar were to translate a nineteenth-century novel that is exactly how it should be rendered. But time has passed and now it is – most resoundingly – a French four-letter word meaning sexual congress considerably more penetrative than a kiss. **Baiser** is therefore discouraged and you are urged to use the more prudent *embrasser* to mean 'kiss'.

---

baklava [Turk] Mediterranean pastry made with honey and
   nuts.
baksheesh [Pers] A tip or gratuity.
bal costumé [Fr] A fancy dress ball.

The language of ballet

The language of ballet is French. They got there first even
though the style of dance itself derived from the Italian
balletto, meaning 'a little dance'. Balletomanes are welcome
to the terms, but in recent years many of these have
overflowed into ordinary writing and conversation. Here are
a few you might meet.

adagio Slow movements to emphasize grace and line. In
   the classic *pas de deux* a partner supports the dancer for
   an even greater display of grace.
allegro Fast movement (opposite of *adagio*) with leaps and
   turns.
arabesque The dancer stands on one leg, the other leg and
   arms extending in the longest possible lines.
ballet d'action [Sp] A ballet that tells a story in
   pantomime.
battement The tapping of one leg with another.
bourrée Very fast little steps that give the illusion of the
   dancer gliding.
cabriole The dancer leaps and taps the lower leg with the
   upper.
écarté A position in which an arm and a leg on the same
   side of the body are extended, almost spreadeagled.
entrechat A leap in which the dancer's legs are quickly
   crossed and uncrossed at the lower calf.
grand jeté A spring from one foot to the other.

jeté A forwards, backwards, or sideways spring.

pirouette A turn on one foot.

sur les pointes On the very tips of the toes.

---

ballon d'essai [Fr] A 'trial balloon' to test opinion.

bal masqué [Fr] A masked ball.

bal musette [Fr] A popular type of dancehall, usually with accordion music.

balti [Urd] Northern Indian cuisine served in cast iron pans.

bambino [It] A young child.

banco [It] A card gambler's offer to place a stake equal to that of the banker.

bandeau [Fr] A ribbon or cloth to bind a woman's hair.

banderilla [Sp] The dart with streamer attached that is thrust into the neck of a bull in bullfighting. The *banderillero* is the bullfighter who places it.

banlieue; banlieues [Fr] The suburbs.

banquette [Fr] Cushioned seat with a cushioned back, especially in restaurants.

banshee [Ir] A wailing female spirit presaging death.

banzai [Jap] Originally a greeting to the Japanese Emperor; a battle cry.

barcarole [Fr] A song of the kind sung by Venetian gondoliers.

bar mitzvah [Heb] (bar-MITS-vuh) Initiation ceremony for Jewish boys. See *bat mitzvah*.

barre [Fr] The waist-high rail around the wall of ballet school practice rooms.

barrette [Fr] hair slide.

barrio [Sp] A ward of a Spanish city or town; Spanish-speaking quarter of a non-Spanish town, especially in the US.

bas bleu [Fr] (bah-bluhr) French equivalent of a bluestocking; a seriously academic woman.

basho [Jap] A sumo wrestling tournament.

bateau-mouche [Fr] Passenger boat on the Seine around Paris.

batiste [Fr] Fine linen or cotton fabric, similar to cambric.

bat mitzvah [Heb] Jewish girl's initiation ceremony into her religious majority at the age of twelve.

batterie de cuisine [Fr] A complete set of cooking utensils.

Bauhaus [Ger] (BOW-howss) Influential Weimar design school (1919-1933) founded by Walter Gropius.

béarnaise [Fr] (bay-uh-NAYS) Widely used sauce made from egg yolks, butter, vinegar and tarragon.

beatae memoriae [Lat] Of blessed memory.

beau geste [Fr] (boh-ZHEST) A magnanimous gesture.

beau idéal [Fr] An ideal of anything in beauty and excellence.

beau monde [Fr] The world of fashion and society.

beauté du diable [Fr] Superficial beauty.

beaux arts [Fr] (boh-ZAR) The fine arts.

beerah [Arab] Beer.

béguin [Fr] Infatuation; a passing fancy.

bel canto [It] Singing in the traditional Italian manner with rich tone, perfect phrasing and clear articulation.

bel esprit [Fr] (bel-es-PREE) A brilliantly witty person.

belle époque [Fr] The prosperous period from the late 1890s to the outbreak of World War I.

belle laide [Fr] See *jolie laide*.

belles-lettres [Fr] Letters or essays that are serious studies, usually of literature, of a critical or philosophical nature.

Benedictus [Lat] God bless you; the part of the Mass that begins (in English) 'Blessed is he that comes in the name of the Lord'.

ben trovato [It] A story or account that, invented or untrue, nevertheless is appropriate anyway. 'Se non e vero, e molto ben trovato' (if it is not true, it is a happy invention).

berceuse [Fr] A cradle song or lullaby.

bergère [Fr] (ber-ZHAIR) A deep, comfortable armchair.

beschlafen Sie es [Ger] Sleep on it; look before you leap.

bête noire [Fr] Someone or something that is especially dreaded and disliked.

bêtise [Fr] A tactless act or remark.

bettschwere [Ger] Without the energy to get out of bed.

bey [Turk] Governor of a Turkish town or district.

bhang [Hindi] Indian hemp.

bibelot [Fr] (BEEB-loh) Small trinket or curio.

bien entendu [Fr] (bih-yahn ah(n)-tah(n)-DOO) Naturally; of course; understood.

bien-pensant [Fr] (bih-yahn pah(n)-sahn) Conformist person holding all the accepted opinions and beliefs.

bien sûr [Fr] (bih-yahn soor) Of course; naturally.

bien trouvé [Fr] (bih-yahn troo-VAY) A happy invention.

bijou [Fr] (BEE-zhoo) Small and beautiful; a trinket.

bijouterie [Fr] (bee-ZHOO-teh-ree) Very delicate jewellery.

Bildungsroman [Ger] A novel about someone's formative experiences.

billabong [Abor] A pool separated from the main stream of a river or creek in Australia.

billet doux [Fr] (bih-lay-DOO) A love-letter.

biru [Jap] Beer.

biretta; berretta [It] Roman Catholic clerical square cap worn by priests (black), bishops (purple), cardinals (red) and other orders (white).

bis dat qui cito dat [Lat] He gives twice who gives quickly; from the aphorism: 'He who gives alms to a poor man quickly, gives it twice'.

bisque [Fr] (beesk) Soup made from shellfish, mainly lobster.

bitterje [Dut] Dutch *jenever* (gin) with bitters.

blague [Fr] Pretentious nonsense; humbug. One who talks such nonsense or boasts is a **blagueur**.

blasé [Fr] (BLAH-zay) Bored and indifferent due to surfeit.

Blaustrumpf [Ger] Bluestocking. See **bas bleu**.

blini seekroy [Rus] Caviar with pancakes.

blitzkrieg [Ger] An intense military attack designed quickly to overwhelm the enemy.

bloembollen [Dut] Bulbs.

Blut ist dicker als Wasser [Ger] Blood is thicker than water.

Blut und Eisen [Ger] Blood and iron: coined by Bismarck.

Boche [Fr] Derogatory term for Germans.

bodega [Sp] (boh-DEG-uh) Wine shop.

bois [Fr] (bwah) Wood; **boiserie** is woodwork.

boîte; boîte de nuit [Fr] (bwaht de nwee) A disreputable club, dancehall or dive; a nightclub.

bolas [Sp] Two or three heavy balls joined by cord. First used by Argentine Gauchos to entangle the legs of cattle to single them out from the herd.

bollenveld [Dut] A bulb field.

bombe surprise [Fr] (bom-soor-PREEZ) A dessert coated to hide its contents; usually ice-cream and meringue.

bonae memoriae [Lat] the pleasant memory of someone.

bona fide [Lat] (adj) (BOH-nuh FYdeh) In good faith; genuine.

bona fides [Lat] (noun) Good faith; honest intention.

bon appétit [Fr] Enjoy your meal.

bon goût [Fr] (boh(n) GOO) Good taste.

bon marché [Fr] (boh(n) MAR-shay) Cheap; also a famous bargain department store in Paris.

bon mot [Fr] (boh(n) MOH) A witty, clever remark.

bonne amie [Fr] (bon-ah-MEE) A close woman friend, who may also be more than just a friend.

bonne à tout faire [Fr] (bon-ah-too-FAIR) A maid-of-all-work.

bonne bouche [Fr] (bon BOOSH) A tasty morsel.

bonne chance [Fr] (bon SHAH(N)S) Good luck!

bon ton [Fr] (boh(n) toh(n)) Sophisticated.

bon vivant [Fr] (boh(n) vee-VAH(N)) A person who enjoys all the luxuries but especially eating and drinking. The term *bon viveur* means the same but is not used in France.

bon voyage [Fr] (boh(n) vwah-YAZH) Have a good journey!

bor [Hun] Wine.

bordel; bordello [It] Brothel. In French *un bordel* is slang for a cock-up, a mess.

bordereau [Fr] A memorandum. The word is indelibly associated with the fake *bordereau* used to convict Dreyfus of treason.

bore da [Welsh] Good morning.

borkostolo [Hun] Wine cellar.

borozo [Hun] Wine bar.

borné [Fr] Narrow-minded; short-sighted.

borsch; borsh; borscht [Rus] Vegetable and beetroot soup widely consumed in Russia and Poland.

bottega [It] A café and wine shop.

bouchée [Fr] (BOO-shay)A small pastry served hot as an hors d'œuvre.

bouclé [Fr] (BOO-klay)A shaggy fabric produced by looped woollen yarn.

bouffant [Fr] (BOO-fah(n)) Puffed-out, back-combed hairstyle.

bouillabaisse [Fr] (boo-yuh-BES) Provençal soup or stew of fish, vegetables and spices.

bouillon [Fr] (BOO-yoh(n)) Thin beef or chicken broth.

boules [Fr] Game played with heavy metal balls tossed at a target ball, usually on a sand court.

boulevardier [Fr] (bool-VAH-dee-ay) A fashionable man who takes care to be seen in all the right places.

bouquet garni [Fr] (boo-kay gar-nih) Bunch of mixed herbs often in sachet-form, used in cooking.

The *bourdalou:* why was a chamber pot named after a priest?

Although not much seen these days, except perhaps in antique shops, the small portable ladies' chamber pot known as a **bourdalou** poses a curious etymological puzzle. It shares its name with the celebrated seventeenth-century Jesuit preacher **Louis Bourdaloue,** but where is the connection? Were his sermons so excruciatingly long-winded?

One theory turns on the design of some early *models,* which had eyes painted on the inside of their bottoms. Father Bourdaloue was the confessor of many of the ladies of the court whose secrets he shared; thus the symbolic all-seeing eye in a most fundamental position. A good try, but the 300-year-old secret of the *bourdalou* seems destined to remain a secret for another three centuries.

Bourse [Fr] (boorss) The French stock exchange in Paris.

braccae tuae aperiuntur [Lat] Your fly is open.

brasserie [Fr] An informal restaurant.

brioche [Fr] (bree-OSH) A small, sweet yeast cake.

brique [Fr] Slang for 10,000 francs.

brise-bise [Fr] A net curtain for the lower half of a window.

broderie anglaise [Fr] Open embroidery on white cotton or fine linen.

brûlé [Fr] Flavoured with burnt sugar; brûler also means to get 'burned' or taken advantage of.

buenas noches [Sp] (BWEY-nas NOH-ches) Goodnight.

buenos días [Sp] (bwey-nos dee-as) Good morning; good-day.

buffo [It] (BOO-foh) Burlesque; comic.

bureau à cylindre [Fr] A roll-top desk.

burn [Scot] A stream.

bushido [Jap] The feudal code of the samurai.

buvette [Fr] Roadside café.

bwana [Swa] Master; form of East African address equivalent to 'Sir'.

Business bloopers

An industrial refrigeration firm once had an international sales director named C. O. Jones. He could be sent anywhere in the world except Spain and Spanish-speaking countries, where the mirth would begin at passport control and not subside until he departed. His name spelt out *cojones*, which is rude Spanish for testicles.

Worldwide businesses have similar problems with their products. Ford couldn't sell its Pinto in Brazil, where the name is Portuguese slang for penis. Rolls Royce couldn't understand why its Silver Mist wasn't moving in Germany until they discovered that to a German 'mist' means manure. The Finns invented a product for de-icing car doors, called it Super Piss, and wondered about slow sales. The sales figures for a particular Spanish potato crisp brand would make interesting reading: it's called Bum.

C

cabaña [Sp] Beach hut.

cabotin [Fr] A show-off; ham actor.

cabriole [Fr] Type of curved furniture leg used from the eighteenth century.

cachou [Fr] (KASH-ooh) Breath-sweetening lozenge.

cacique [Sp] Originally an American Indian chief in Spanish-speaking regions; now used to mean local political boss.

cacoethes loquendi [Lat] (kah-koh-EETH-ees loh-KWEN-dee) An irresistible urge to talk. *Cacoethes scribendi* is a compulsive urge to write.

cadeau [Fr] (KAH-doh) A gift.

cadit quaestio [Lat] There is nothing more to discuss.

caeteris paribus [Lat] Other things being equal.

café [Fr] (kaff-ay) Coffee. *Café au lait* (kaff-ay-oh-LAY) – coffee with milk; *Café crème* – white coffee; *café noir* – black coffee.

cahier [Fr] (kah-yeh(r)) Originally a notebook; a written or printed report of a meeting or conference.

camino real [Sp] The best way to achieve a result.

campo santo [It] A burial ground.

canaille [Fr] (kan-EYE) The crowd, the mob, *hoi polloi*.

canapé [Fr] (KAN-uh-pay) Small slice of bread or toast with a savoury topping.

ça ne fait rien [Fr] It is of no importance.

cantina [Sp] Bar or wine shop.

capable de tout [Fr] Unpredictable in behaviour; likely to stop at nothing.

capo d'opera [It] A masterpiece.

caporal [Fr] Type of light tobacco.

capote anglaise [Fr] English hood, a Gallic tilt at the French letter, French slang for condom.

carabiniere [It] (karah-bin-YAIR-ih) Armed Italian policeman.

caramba [Sp] A rare exclamation.

caret [Lat] Symbol (λ), an insertion mark used to indicate that something is missing in written or printed matter.

carità pelosa [It] Literally, hairy generosity: generosity with some ulterior motive.

carnet [Fr] (KAR-nay) Small booklet, usually a document.

carpe diem [Lat] (KAR-pay DEE-em) Make the most of today; eat, drink and be merry for tomorrow we die.

carreras de caballos [Sp] Horse-racing.

carretera [Sp] Road; highway.

carte blanche [Fr] (kart BLAH(N)SH) Complete freedom and authority; full discretionary power.

carte de visite [Fr] Small nineteenth-century visiting cards.

carte d'identité [Fr] Identity card.

cartonnier [Fr] Cabinet with flat drawers for storing prints, drawings and plans.

cartouche [Fr] Inscription on an ornamental scroll.

casa [It] A villa or detached house.

ça saute aux yeux [Fr] It's obvious; it cannot be missed.

cassis [Fr] (kah-SEESS) Syrupy blackcurrant cordial.

cassoulet [Fr] A meat and bean dish.

casus belli [Lat] An event used to justify a war or quarrel.

catachresis [Lat from Gk] (kat-uk-KREE-sis) The misuse of words.

catalogue raisonné [Fr] (KAT-uh-log RAY-zon-ay)
Systematic descriptive listing, usually of a collection or
an artist's work.

catholicon [Gk] A panacea; universal remedy.

caudillo [Sp] (kow-DEE-yoh) A military or political leader
in a Spanish-speaking country.

cause célèbre [Fr] (KAUZ se-LEB-ruh) A famous trial,
lawsuit or controversy.

causerie [Fr] A chatty literary essay or discussion.

ça va? [Fr] (sah-VAH) Everything OK?

ça va sans dire [Fr] That is obvious; it goes without
saying.

cave [Lat] (KA-vih) Slang for 'Look out!'; 'Beware!'.

caveat [Lat] 'Let him beware'; a warning or caution.

caveat emptor [Lat] 'Let the buyer beware'; a warning
that it is the buyer, not the seller, who must take the
risk.

cavoli riscaldati [It] Literally, 'reheated cabbage'. A lapsed
love affair, difficult to revive.

céad mile fáilte [Ir] Irish welcome: 'A hundred thousand
welcomes!'.

ceilidh [Gael] (KAY-lee) An entertainment in Scotland and
Ireland, usually consisting of dancing, folk music,
singing – and talking.

cercare il pelo nell'uovo [It] To seek the hair in the egg;
to pick faults where none exists.

cerveja [Port] Beer.

cerveza [Sp] Beer.

c'est la guerre [Fr] (say-lah-GAIR) That's war; it happens.

c'est la vie [Fr] (say-la-vee) That's life.

ceud mile fàilte [Gael] (kood meel-uh FAL-chuh) Scottish
Gaelic welcome: 'A hundred thousand welcomes!'

ch'a [Ch] Tea. The British slang term is **char**.

chacun à son goût [Fr] (shah-kuh(n)-ah-soh(n)-GOO)
Everyone to their own taste.

chacun à son métier [Fr] (shah-kuh(n)-ah-soh(n)-may-tyay) Everyone to their own trade.

chacun pour soi [Fr] (shah-kuh(n) poor SWAHR) Everyone for themselves.

chagrin d'amour [Fr] Misery from an unhappy love affair.

chaise-longue [Fr] (shayz-lor(ng)) Sofa with back and one end open.

chambrer [Fr] (SHAHM-bray) To bring a wine to room temperature.

chamise [Jap] Tea-house.

Changcheng [Ch] The Great Wall of China.

Changjiang [Ch] The Yangtse River.

chapati; chapatti [Hindi] Flat cake of unleavened bread.

charcuterie [Fr] Shop selling cooked meat; cold cuts of pork.

chargé d'affaires [Fr] (shar-zhay da-FAIR) Diplomatic representative below the rank of ambassador.

charivari [Fr] A demonstrative racket or celebration.

charpoy [Urdu] Indian bed, usually of woven hemp.

chasse [Fr] (shass) A liqueur following coffee.

Châteaubriand [Fr] (sha-toh-BREE-ah(n)) Thick steak cut from a fillet of beef.

chaud-froid [Fr] (shoh-frwah) Cold meat or chicken covered with a savoury jellied sauce.

chef de mission [Fr] Organizer or leader of a team.

chef d'équipe [Fr] Manager of a team.

chef d'œuvre [Fr] (shay DURV-ruh) A masterpiece.

chemin de fer [Fr] A game of cards like baccarat.

cheongsam [Ch] A long straight oriental dress with a high collar and a slit on one side of the skirt.

cherchez la femme [Fr] (shair-shay la fam) 'Look for the woman'; there's always a woman involved.

chère amie [Fr] (shair ah-MEE) A mistress or sweetheart.

chéri(e) [Fr] (sheh-REE) Darling of *mon chéri, ma chérie*

che sarà sarà [It] (kay-suh-RAH-suh-RAH) What will be, will be.

chevaux de frise [Fr] Iron spikes or some other sharp deterrent on the tops of fences and walls.

chez [Fr] (shay) At the house of – e.g.: *Chez Humperdinck*.

chez moi [Fr] (shay MWAH) At my house.

chez nous [Fr] (shay NOO) At our house.

chiasse [Fr] Slang term for 'the runs' induced by fear.

chi bestia va a Roma bestia ritorna [It] He that goes to Rome a fool returns a fool.

chicane [Fr] Series of sharp, narrow bends used on a motor racing circuit or public road to slow speeding vehicles.

chignon [Fr] (SHEE-nyo(n)) The roll or coil of hair at the back of a woman's head.

chikatet [Jap] Japanese underground railway systems.

chin-chin; ch'ing ch'ing [Ch] Informal greeting, farewell or toast.

The challenge of Chinese

Chinese is the language of one billion people, and is thus the most-used language in the world. But many of those billion users can't understand one another; while written Chinese is standard, spoken Chinese comes in several varieties which are mutually unintelligible. The main and official dialect is Mandarin but huge numbers of the population (including Singapore Chinese) speak Cantonese.

The written language remains a closed book to most westerners but the notion of phonetically spelling out Chinese with Roman characters – called **Pinyin** – has helped to make the spoken language easier to handle. Well, a bit easier: if you manage to máster the pronunciation system you are then faced with the four tones – for spoken Chinese is above all a tonal language. The character **ma,** if spoken with the first tone, means 'mother'; the same character spoken with the third tone means 'horse'. If you intend to tackle Chinese, be prepared for glorious confusion!

You will also have noticed that many English spellings, particularly of place names, have been changed in recent years so that they read roughly how they sound in Mandarin: Peking to **Beijing**; Mao Tse-tung to **Mao Zedong**; Canton to **Guangzhou**, and so on.

---

chronique scandaleuse [Fr] A scandalous story or gossip.

chuddar [Hindi] A garment worn by Muslim women that covers them from head to foot.

chun jie [Ch] Chinese New Year.

chutzpah [Yidd] Shameless audacity; cheek.

ciabatta [It] (chah-BAT-tah) slipper; bread made with olive oil.

ciao [It] (chow) Hello; goodbye.

cicerone [It] A guide, especially at sites of antiquities.

ci-devant [Fr] Formerly; that which used to be.

cinéma-vérité [Fr] A style of making films in which the aim is to make the result look as much like real life as possible.

cinquecento [It] (ching-kweh-CHEN-toh) The period from 1500 to 1600.

circa [Lat] (SER-kuh) Approximately; at the approximate time of. Abbreviated to **c** or **ca** and used before a date: **c1990**.

ciré [Fr] (see-ray) Smooth, usually waxed, fabric

clachan [Gael] Rural village in the Scottish West Highlands.

claque [Fr] (klak) Originally a group hired to applaud in a theatre; now used in a derogatory way to describe a group of sycophants blindly applauding their leader. Such people are *claqueurs*.

cocotte [Fr] Prostitute; also a fireproof cooking dish.

cognoscenti [It] (kon-yoh-SHEN-tih) People who are in the know about something; connoisseurs.

coitus interruptus [Lat] Contraception method involving withdrawal during sexual intercourse. In Australia it is called 'Getting off at Redfern' (the station just before the terminus, Sydney Central).

colleen [Ir] A girl or young woman.

Comédie Française [Fr] The French national theatre in Paris.

comédie humaine [Fr] (kom-uh-dee ooh-MEN) The comedy of life. *La Comédie Humaine* is the title of Balzac's fictional social history of France.

comédie noire [Fr] (kom-uh-dee nwahr) Black comedy.

comme ci, comme ça [Fr] Neither good nor bad; so-so.

commedia dell'arte [It] (kom-ay-dyah del-AH-tay) The well-known characters of Columbine, Harlequin and Punchinello are from this stylised Italian comedy genre established in the sixteenth century.

comme il faut [Fr] (kom eel FOH) Correct; how things are done; in accordance with acceptable manners.

commère [Fr] A female *compère*.

commis [Fr] (kom-mih) An assistant or apprentice waiter or chef.

commune [Fr] The smallest administrative division in France (also in Belgium, Switzerland and Italy), governed by a mayor and council.

compère [Fr] The host or commentator of an entertainment, contest or programme. See *commère*.

compos mentis [Lat] Sane; of sound mind. See *non compos mentis*.

con amore [It] Music to be performed lovingly.

con brio [It] Music with energy; to be performed with spirit.

concours d'élégance [Fr] (koh(n)-koor day-lay-gah(n)s) Beauty parade of vintage, veteran or exotic motor cars.

confrère [Fr] (KO(N)-frair) A professional colleague.

connard [Fr] Extremely rude expression for a fool, an idiot, someone stupid or dumb.

consommé [Fr] (kohn-SOH-may) Clear meat or chicken soup.

contra mundum [Lat] Against the world; in the face of accepted wisdom.

contrat social [Fr] (ko(n)-trah soh-SYAL) The surrender of certain personal liberties to the community in return for an organised society (from title of a book by the philospher Jean-Jacques Rousseua)

contretemps [Fr] A small disagreement.

conversazione [It] (kon-ver-sat-sih-OH-nay) A social gathering at which people discuss the arts or literature.

coq au vin [Fr] (kok oh VAH(N)) Chicken cooked in red wine.

coquilles St Jacques [Fr] (koh-kee sah(n) ZHAHK) Scallops cooked in sauce and served in scallop shells.

coram populo [Lat] In full view of the people; in public.

cordon bleu [Fr] (kor-doh(n) BLUR) Meaning the blue ribbon; a very high distinction; first-rate; food prepared to the highest culinary standards.

cordon sanitaire [Fr] A buffer zone or boundary to keep a danger at bay, such as an infectious disease or enemy power.

corniche [Fr] (kor-NEESH) Coastal road, typically cut into steep mountains. The road between Nice and Monte Carlo is a famous example.

cornuto [It] Literally, 'horned'. A male insult to another, implying he has been cuckolded. Even worse, *cornuto e contento* – happy cuckold.

corps d'élite [Fr] (kor day-LEET) People who are the best at something; crack corps.

Corpus Christi [Lat] The festival of the Blessed Sacrament or Holy Eucharist.

corpus delicti [Lat] The sum of the facts that constitute an offence in law. Often incorrectly used to describe the corpse or body in connection with a crime.

corrida; corrida de toros [Sp] Bullfight; the running of bulls.

CORRIDA: THE RUNNING OF THE BULLS

corroboree [Aust Abor] (koh-ROB-uh-ree) Australian Aboriginal dance ceremony.

cortège [Fr] (kor-TEZH) A procession, especially one following a funeral.

Cosa Nostra [It] U.S. branch of the Sicilian Mafia, meaning 'our thing'.

Così fan tutte, ossia la scuola degli amanti [It] All women do it; that is the way of all women, or *The School for Lovers*, Mozart's opera.

Côte d'Azur [Fr] (koht dah-ZOOR) The French Riviera.

Côte de Beaune [Fr] (koht duh-BONE) Southern part of the Côte d'Or Burgundy region from Dijon to Nuits-St-Georges.

Côte d'Or [Fr] (KOHT dor) The Burgundy region of France, 300 km southeast of Paris.

côtelette [Fr] A chop or cutlet.

couilles [Fr] Testicles. Used commonly and vulgarly and
with infinite variety. **Mes couilles!** – bollocks!

coulant [Fr] Easy-going; easy to get on with.

couleur de temps [Fr] Whichever way the wind blows;
according to circumstances.

Countries, cities and place-names

For a century and a half the British have freely anglicised
foreign place-names. If you asked a citizen of Beijing (we've
perversely called it Peking for generations) if you were in
China you'd be met with an uncomprehending stare; there
the country is called **Zhongghuó.** We say Athens and
Corfu; the Greeks say – and they should know – **Athena**
and **Kerkira.** The country we know as Sweden is really
Sverige; Brussels is **Bruxelles**; Italy is **Italia**; Hungary is
Magyarország where, to be fair, they call Great Britain
Nagy-Britannia.

But, slowly, English speakers are becoming more
internationalised, and many of us can now work out that
Firenze is Florence, **Köbenhavn** is Copenhagen and
München is Munich.

---

coup de foudre [Fr] (koo duh FOOD-ruh) Love at first
sight; a sudden and surprising event.

coup de grâce [Fr] (koo duh GRAHS) A final and decisive
stroke; a mortal blow that ends a victim's suffering.

coup de main [Fr] (koo duh MA(N)) A surprise attack.

coup d'essai [Fr] (koo day-SAY) A trial or first attempt.

coup d'état [Fr] (koo day-TAH) A violent seizure of power,
usually the illegal overturning of a government.

coup de maître [Fr] (koo duh MEHtruh) A masterstroke;
performance worthy of a master.

coup de théâtre [Fr] (koo duh tay-ART-ruh) A sudden
and dramatic action; a sensational stage success.

coup d'œil [Fr] (koo DUH-ee) A quick glance; comprehensive view taken by a quick glance.

coureur (de jupons) [Fr] A skirt-chaser; a womaniser.

couscous [Fr from Arab **kouskous**] Spicy North African dish of steamed semolina served with stew.

coûte que coûte [Fr] (koot kuh koot) No matter what the cost; at all costs.

couvert [Fr] A set place at a meal table; a restaurant 'cover' for which a charge is made.

craquelure [Fr] Crazing on the surface of old oil paintings and on pottery glazing.

crème de la crème [Fr] (krem-duh-lah-KREM) Cream of the cream; the very best.

cri de cœur [Fr] (kree duh kur) A cry from the heart.

crime passionnel [Fr] (kreem pass-yuh-NEL) A crime motivated by the passions: often murder, usually sexual passion.

crise de conscience [Fr] An attack of moral doubt; an awakening of one's scruples.

crise de cœur [Fr] An emotional crisis; a catastrophic love affair.

crise de nerfs [Fr] (krees duh NAIR) A hysterical attack; a brief nervous breakdown.

Croix de Guerre [Fr] (krwah duh GAIR) French military decoration for gallantry first awarded in 1915.

croûte [Fr] (kroot) Crust; fried bread used as a base for savouries.

croûtons [Fr] (kroo-TOH(N)) Cubes of toasted or fried bread usually served in soup.

crudités [Fr] (KROO-dee-tay) Appetiser of sliced, raw mixed vegetables served with dips or sauces.

csarda [Hun] (char-duh) A country inn.

csárdás; czárdás [Hun] (char-duh) Hungarian national dance.

¡cuéntaselo a tu abuela! [Sp] Tell that to your grandmother!

cui bono? [Lat] (kwee BOH-noh) For whose benefit? Who will profit by it?

cui malo? [Lat] (kwee MAH-loh) Whom will it harm?

cum grano salis [Lat] With a grain of salt; not to be taken literally; treat with caution.

cum laude [Lat] (kum LOW-day) With praise; an above-average examination pass; a pass with distinction. (See also *magna cum laude* and *summa cum laude*).

curé [Fr] (KYOOR-ray) French parish priest.

currente calamo [Lat] Writing that is dashed off without pause.

curriculum vitae [Lat] Abbreviation *CV*. An outline of someone's educational and professional history, usually submitted with a job application.

cwm [Welsh] (koom) A valley.

Cymraeg [Welsh] (kuhm-RA-eeg) The Welsh language.

Cymru [Welsh] (KUHM-ree) Wales.

Cymry [Welsh] (KUHM-ree) The Welsh people.

D

dacha [Rus] (DAH-tshuh) Russian country house or villa.
Dáil [Ir] (doyl) Parliament of the Irish Republic in Dublin.
damnosa hereditas [Lat] A disastrous inheritance; one
 that brings problems rather than benefits.
da multos annos [Lat] A wish for someone's long life.

Danish and *Nudansk*

Danish, or one of the many versions of it, such as *Nudansk*
('new Danish'), is spoken by five million Danes, many of
whom are on excellent terms with English. But their own
language, developed over a millennium, is colourful. Here
are a couple of samples; there are no prizes for identifying
the English versions of these two famous lines, both linked
to a Shakespearian brush with Denmark four centuries ago:

● *Der er noget råddent I Danmark rige.*
● *Lykken er en cigar, der hedder Hamlet.*

Answers on page 43

---

danke schön [Ger] (dank-kuh shern) Thank you very
 much.
danse du ventre [Fr] Variety of belly dancing.
danse macabre [Fr] (dah(n)s muh-KARB-ruh) The dance
 of death.

darunter und darüber [Ger] Topsy-turvy.

Das fragt sich [Ger] That remains to be seen.

Das kleinste Haar wirft seinen Schatten [Ger] The smallest hair casts a shadow. Attributed to Goethe.

de bene esse [Lat] Subject to certain conditions; without prejudice; provisionally.

déboutonné; déboutonnée [Fr] Unbuttoned; careless; sloppy.

déclassé [Fr] Having lost one's social status.

décolletage [Fr] (day-kol-TAHZH) A revealing low-cut neckline on a woman's dress. **Décolleté** describes a garment having such a neckline.

de die in diem [Lat] From day to day.

de facto [Lat] (day FAK-toh) In reality; in fact.

défense d'entrer [Fr] (day-fah(n)s dah(n)-tray) No entry.

défense de fumer [Fr] (day-fah(n)s duh-foo-may) No smoking.

dégagé [Fr] (day-gah-zhay) Relaxed; unconstrained; detached.

dégueulasse [Fr] Disgusting. Used vulgarly: *c'est un dégueulasse!* – he's a rotten sod!

de gustibus (non est disputandum) [Lat] There's no accounting for tastes.

de haut en bas [Fr] (duh oh ah(n) BAH) Consciously superior; in a condescending way.

Dei Gratia [Lat] By the grace of God.

déjà vu [Fr] The feeling or conviction that an experience is being repeated: a journey, a place revisited, an event, etc.

de jure [Lat] (day YOO-ray) In law; by right, but not necessarily happening.

delineavit; del [Lat] (He/she) drew it. Used with the name of the artist: Hogarth *del.*

Danish Answers

The two lines, translated, are:

- 'Something is rotten in the state of Denmark,' and
- 'Happiness is a cigar called Hamlet'.

---

delirium tremens [Lat] In slang, *the DT's*. Psychotic condition exhibiting delirium, tremor and hallucinations, induced by excessive intake of alcohol.

démarche [Fr] (day-mahsh) A new move in political or diplomatic affairs.

demi-mondaine [Fr] A woman of the *demi-monde*, of low repute.

demi-pension [Fr] Half-board, ie bed, breakfast and one main meal.

demi-tasse [Fr] A small coffee cup; a small cup of coffee.

démodé [Fr] Outdated, or no longer fashionable.

démon de midi [Fr] Reawakening of sexual appetite in middle-age.

de mortuis (nil nisi bonum) [Lat] Say nothing bad about the dead.

de nos jours [Fr] (duh noh zhoor) Of our time. Used after a name: 'She was the George Sand *de nos jours*'.

dénouement [Fr] (day-NOO-moh(n)) The unravelling of a mystery and its solution.

de nouveau [Fr] (duh noo-voh) Again; once more.

Deo gratias [Lat] Thanks to God.

Deo Optimo Maximo [Fr] To God the greatest. Motto of the Benedictine order; the initials DOM are seen on the labels of Benedictine liqueur.

Deo volente; abbrev. *DV* [Lat] God willing; unless something prevents it.

dépaysé [Fr] (day-pay-zay) Disoriented; like a fish out of water.

de profundis [Lat] (A cry) from the depths of despair. The first two words of the Latin version of Psalm 130 and the title of Oscar Wilde's apologia published in 1905.

département [Fr] (day-pahrt-moh(n)) One of the administrative divisions of France.

dépaysé [Fr] (day-pay-zay) Disoriented; feeling out of place.

député [Fr] (day-puh-tay) Member of the French lower house of parliament.

dérailler [Fr] Slang for 'to go off the rails'.

de règle [Fr] (duh REHG-luh) Required by rule or convention.

der ewige Jude [Ger] The eternal Jew.

de rigeur [Fr] (duh-rih-GUR) Required by etiquette.

dernier cri [Fr] (der-nyay kree) Latest fashion; trendy.

dernier ressort [Fr] A last resort.

derrière [Fr] Buttocks; backside.

der Schuster hat die schlechtesten Schuhe [Ger] The cobbler's children are always the worst shod.

déshabillé [Fr] (day-za-BEE-yay) In a state of undress; a dressing-gown.

désœuvré [Fr] (day-zoo-vray) Idle; not doing anything.

détente [Fr] (day-TAH(N)T) Relaxation of a state of tension, usually between two countries.

détraqué [Fr] Unbalanced; insane; out of order.

de trop [Fr] (duh troh) Superfluous or unwanted.

deus ex machina [Lat] (DAY-uhs eks MAK-ee-nuh) A god or unlikely character who appears, in a play or novel, to solve the mystery or resolve the plot.

Deus vobiscum [Lat] God be with you.

Deuxième Bureau [Fr] French counterpart of Britain's MI5, the Military Intelligence Department.

dharma [Hindi] Social custom that is religious and moral duty in Hinduism. For Buddhists it is the truth as taught by Buddha.

dharna [Hindi] The practice of obtaining justice by sitting or fasting on the doorstep of the home of the offender.

dhobi [Hindi] Λ washerman or washerwoman in India.

dhoti [Hindi] Male loincloth as worn in India.

dialogue de sourds [Fr] Discussion in which neither party listens to the other.

Diaspora [Gk] The dispersion of the Jews from ancient Palestine 597-538 BC.

Dies Irae [Lat] Day of wrath. Judgment Day; a hymn describing this.

Dieu et mon droit [Fr] (DYUR ay mo(n) DRWAH) God and my right. The motto of the Royal Arms of Great Britain.

Directoire [Fr] (dih-rek-TWAHR) The fashions of the French Directory period, 1795-9, following classical lines which in turn inspired English Regency fashions.

dirigisme [Fr] State control of an economy or society.

dirndl [Ger] (durn-duhl) Alpine peasant-style dress with full gathered skirt, tight waist and bodice, and blouse with short puffed sleeves.

dis aliter visum [Lat] The gods decided otherwise.

disjecta membra [Lat] Scattered fragments of a writer's literary work.

distingué [Fr] (dees-TAH(N)-gay) Distinguished in manner and appearance.

djellabah *see also* **jellaba** [Arab] Hooded cloak with wide sleeves worn in North Africa.

djibbah [Arab] Long open coat worn by Muslims.

djinn [Arab] Spirit in Muslim mythology able to assume human and animal form. Sometimes spelt *jinnee, jinni*.

dolce far niente [It] Enjoyable idleness.

dolce vita [It] (DOL-chay VEE-tah) Life of luxury and sensuality.

dolmades; dolmathes [Gk] Traditional Greek dish of vine leaves stuffed with savoury rice.

Dominus illuminatio mea [Lat] The Lord is my light. Motto of Oxford University.

donné [Fr] A basic assumption; accepted fact.

Donner und Blitzen [Ger] Thunder and lightning. An expression of amazement.

doppelgänger [Ger] An apparition identical to a living person.

douane [Fr] (dwan) Customs office.

douanier [Fr] (DWAN-yay) Customs officer.

double entendre [Fr] (doo-blah(n)-TAH(N)-druh) A word or phrase having two interpretations, one of them indelicate. The phrase **double entente** is used in France instead.

drachenfutter Literally, 'dragonfodder'. A guilty husband's present to his wife.

droit de cité [Fr] Freedom of a city, club or organization.

droit de seigneur [Fr] In feudal times, the right of a lord to sleep with his tenant's bride on her wedding night.

Duae tabulae rasae in quibus nihil scriptum est [Lat] 'Two minds without a single thought' – the motto of movie comedians Laurel and Hardy.

d'un certain age [Fr] Euphemism for 'middle aged'.

Dutch dung

British tourists in Holland are often taken aback by the wide and frequent use there of the expletive **shit.** The word was borrowed from English but to the Dutch it is the mildest of epithets and as meaningless as **gee, blimey** or **gosh.** It's a phenomenon of language borrowing that a word weighed down with vulgarity in one country may be merely an amusing trifle in another. A century or so ago the English borrowed such a word from the Dutch. We know it as **poppycock;** they know it as *pappekak,* which means 'soft shit'.

---

dydd da [Welsh] Good day!

E

eau-de-nil [Fr] (oh-duh-NEEL) A tint of pale green.

eau-de-vie [Fr] Literally, 'water of life'; any strong liqueur or spirit.

ébauche [Fr] (ay-bohsh) A writer's rough outline for a novel; a quick sketch.

Ecce Homo [Lat] (ek-kee hoh-moh) 'Behold the man'; The image of Christ crowned with thorns.

ecce lacunar mirum! [Lat] 'Now, that's a ceiling!'; to be murmured approvingly in the Sistine Chapel.

echt [Ger] Genuine; pure; unadulterated.

éclair [Fr] A chocolate-covered, cream-filled small pastry.

éclaircissement [Fr] (ay-klair-sees-mah(n)) A revelation; an explanation.

éclat [Fr] (ay-KLAH) A great success; a dazzling effect.

école [Fr] (ay-KOL) A school; a group of artistic disciples.

écrase! [Fr] Shut up!

écritoire [Fr] (ay-krih-TWAHR) Writing desk.

écrivain maudit [Fr] (ay-krih-va(h)n moh-dee) Accursed, or damned, writer.

écru [Fr] (ay-kroo) Greyish-yellow; the colour of unbleached linen.

écurie [Fr] (ay-kyoo-REE) A works motor racing team.

Edelweiss [Ger] Small white Alpine flowering plant.

editio princeps [Lat] The first printed copy of a book.

eekra [Rus] Caviar.

Effendi [Turk] An important person; a gentleman.

egeszsegeunkre! [Hun] Cheers!

Egri Bikaver [Hun] Bull's Blood red wine.

eine Schwalbe macht keinen Sommer [Ger] One swallow doesn't make a summer.

ein unmütz Leben ist ein früher Tod [Ger] A wasted life is premature death (Goethe).

eisteddfod [Welsh] (aye-STETH-vod) Welsh cultural festival.

élan [Fr] (ay-lah(n)) Vivacity; style and vigour.

Elatha [Gk] Greece.

eldorado; El Dorado [Sp] A place of fabled opportunity; the fabled South American city of immense riches.

elinikos kafes [Gk] Greek coffee.

embarras de choix [Fr] So many options it's difficult to make a choice.

embarras de richesses [Fr] Embarrassment of riches; so many options to choose from.

embonpoint [Fr] (ah(n)-bo(n)-pwah(n)) Attractive plumpness.

embouchure [Fr] (ah(m)-boo-SHOOR) The correct application of the lips and tongue when playing a wind instrument.

emeritus [Lat] Retired, but retaining the title, often on an honorary basis. Usually, an emeritus professor.

éminence grise [Fr] (eh-meen-ah(n)s GREEZ) Literally, 'grey eminence'. Someone who wields considerable power behind the scenes.

empressement [Fr] Enthusiastic display of cordiality.

en avant [Fr] (ah(n) ah-VAH(N)) Move ahead! Forward!

en bloc [Fr] (ah(n)-BLOK) In a body; all together.

en brochette [Fr] Food grilled on a skewer.

en brosse [Fr] (ah(n) BROS) Hair cut short and bristly. In Britain, once referred to as the 'bog-brush' style.

en cabochon [Fr] Describes a gem that is rounded and

polished but does not have facets cut in it.

enceinte [Fr] (ah(n)-SAH(N)T) Pregnant.

enchiridion [Gk] A handbook; manual, work of reference.

enculé [Fr] A very vulgar insult, equivalent to bugger or sod.

endimanché [Fr] Dressed in Sunday best.

en famille [Fr] (ah(n) fah-MEE-uh) As one of the family; informal.

enfant chérie [Fr] A favoured, pampered child.

enfant gâté [Fr] A spoiled child; an adult who behaves like a spoiled child.

enfant terrible [Fr] (ah(n)-fah(n) teh-REEB-luh) Someone who embarrasses by being unconventional, indiscreet, opinionated and loud.

en fête [Fr] In festive mood.

en garde [Fr] On guard; a call to a fencer to adopt a defensive stance; in readiness for attack.

English found wanting

Here's a letter to *The Times* complaining about the elitist use of foreign words in the paper:

"Sir, Your leading article of November 30 tells us that 'The attitude of 'L'état, c'est moi' is an affliction that comes . . .'"

'Some of your readers would not know what this means.

'I am one of them and I have been reading your newspaper for over 30 years. Of course, I can guess fairly accurately; I have seen the phrase before and having looked it up in the back of my dictionary, find that I was just about right.

'Even [Bernard] Levin, for a change, managed to get through an article on the opposite page without resorting to bits of Latin, etc, in italics. I wonder if all your own staff can unhesitatingly read through these foreign phrases and know what they mean better than if they were written in English.

'I don't share John Major's wish for a classless society, but as they are, your articles are for that class of people who were taught French, Latin or whatever language you decide to make use of.'

The letter ran without editorial comment, but a week later another reader replied:

'Sir, [The letter of December 3] highlights the prejudices that many people still maintain towards foreign languages. There are certain phrases which in their source language are far more graphic, concise and eleoquent than if they are translated.

'Are we to emasculate our language to such a point that any phrases which might be considered difficult or elitist should be banned? Why stop at foreign phrases? We would soon be at a nadir of linguistic expression unmatched even by Enid Blyton.

'The richness of any language develops from its history and its contact with other countries and their language and literature. It is high time that we all realise this.'

---

en l'air [Fr] Up in the air; vague; left for discussion.

en masse [Fr] All at once; in a group.

en öl [Swed] (AN URL) Beer.

en passant [Fr] (ah(n) pas-SAH(N)) In passing; a chess move for capturing a pawn.

en paz descanse [Sp] May he rest in peace.

en pension [Fr] Living in lodgings as a boarder.

en plein air [Fr] (ah(n) plen) In the open air.

en plus [Fr] (ah(n) PLOOS) In addition.

en principe [Fr] A very common colloquial expression roughly meaning 'in theory' or 'as a rule' but conveying a strong note of scepticism.

en rapport [Fr] (ah(n) rah-por) In sympathy; in harmony.

en revanche [Fr] In return; as an act of retaliation.

entente cordiale [Fr] (ah(n)-TAH(N)T kor-DYAHL) A friendly understanding between countries.

en-tout-cas [Fr] (ah(n) too KAH) An umbrella-style sunshade.

entr'acte [Fr] (AH(N)-trakt) Interval between theatrical acts.

entrecôte [Fr] Tenderloin or rib steak.

entre deux guerres [Fr] The period between World War I and World War II.

Entre-Deux-Mers [Fr] (ah(n)-truh dur mair) Large wine area of the Gironde, between the Dordogne and Garonne rivers.

entre la espada y la pared [Sp] Literally, between the sword and the wall. Means 'between the devil and the deep blue sea'.

entremets [Fr] (ah(n)-truh-may) Side dish served between the main courses of a meal.

entre nous [Fr] Between ourselves; in strict confidence.

entrepôt [Fr] (ah(n)-truh-po) A commercial warehouse; a trading centre or port.

en un clin d'œil [Fr] In the twinkling of an eye.

en villégiature [Fr] Holidaying or staying in the country.

épatant [Fr] (ay-pah-tah(n)) Astounding; mind-boggling.

e pluribus unum [Lat] One out of the many. The motto of the USA.

épris [Fr] In love; enamoured.

è pur troppo vero [It] It is only too true.

eretz ha-kodesh [Heb] Holy Land.

eretz Israel [Heb] The modern state of Israel.

ergo [Lat] Therefore; hence.

Er hat Bohnen in den Ohren [Ger] He has beans in his ears; none are so deaf as those who will not listen.

Er hat Haare auf den Zähnen [Ger] He has hairs on his teeth; he is a sharp one.

Erin go bragh; Eire go brath [Ir] Ireland forever!

ersatz [Ger] A poor imitation; an inferior substitute.

erwtensoep [Dut] Favourite Dutch dish of thick pea soup with smoked sausage, pork fat and pig's knuckle.

escándalo [Sp] A scandal; a fuss.

escargots [Fr] (es-kar-goh) Edible snails.

es fällt keine Eiche von einem Streiche [Ger] You can't fell an oak with a single stroke.

es ist nicht alles Gold, was glänzt [Ger] All is not gold that glitters.

es una trampa [Sp] It's a fix! Often shouted at sporting events.

espadrille [Fr] (es-pah-dreel) Casual rope-soled canvas shoe.

esprit de corps [Fr] Pride in belonging to a group; a shared sense of fellowship, loyalty and purpose.

esprit de l'escalier [Fr] (es-pree duh les-KAHL-yay) The brilliant remark that one thinks of too late.

esprit fort [Fr] (es-pree FOR) An independent thinker.

es regnet in Strömen [Ger] It's pouring with rain.

es stirbt als Knabe, wen die Götter lieben [Ger] Those whom the gods love die young.

estaminet [Fr] (es-TA-mee-nay) Small bar especially in the context of the First World War.

est deus in nobis [Lat] There is a god within us. (Ovid)

estiatorion [Gk] In Greece, an ordinary restaurant.

étagère [Fr] Hanging set of shelves or bookshelves.

et alii [Lat] And others; and other things. Abbreviation *et al*.

état d'âme [Fr] The state of the soul; how a person feels deep down.

et cetera [Lat]; And other things (the rest); and so on. Sometimes abbreviated to **etc.** or expressed as one word.

étoile [Fr] (ay-TWAHL) Star; star-shaped.

être cousu d'argent [Fr] To be rolling in money.

et sequentia; et seq [Lat] And the following.

et tu, Brute! [Lat] (et TOO BROO-tay) 'And you Brutus!' Allegedly Caesar's last words when he saw Brutus among his assassins. Used ever since to reproach a friend who betrays.

étude [Fr] (eh-TOOD) A short musical composition to highlight the technical virtuosity of a soloist.

eureka [Gk] 'I have found it!' said Archimedes upon discovering the principle of specific gravity. Now used as an expression of delight in finding the answer to a problem.

Europäische Wirtschafts Gemeinschaft [Ger] European Economic Community.

Europäische Union [Ger] European Union.

Eurospeak

When **discothèque** crossed the Channel it seemed an innocent enough borrowing. The French certainly didn't mind, but some disapprove of what they received in return: an unstoppable jargon that has, over the past three decades, travelled to the far frontiers of Europe, where the French relax in *un living* (living room) and wish each other *bon weekend!* Russians kick off their *shoozy* and play *diskis*, Italians listen to their *rockmen* and *long playings* while the Germans go out *joggen*.

English has for some time been Europe's preferred second language. Most Danes speak it fluently, as do large numbers of Dutch and Belgians; 80% of French and German secondary pupils study it. But many Europeans resent the infiltration of unnecessary English words and phrases into their languages to create *franglais* (*see article, page* 62), *itangliano, swinglish* and other hybrids. As *Pravda* once reported, the phenomenon was a *seriosnaya situasia* and a *nationalnaya problema.*

événement [Fr] Event, occurrence, result; climax.

Ewigkeit [Ger] Thin air; eternity; the unknown.

ex cathedra [Lat] With unquestioned authority; infallible.

exceptis excipiendis [Lat] When the appropriate exceptions have been made.

exempli gratia; e.g. [Lat] For example.

exeunt [Lat] A stage direction meaning 'they go out'.

ex granis fit acervus [Lat] Many grains make a heap; every little helps.

ex gratia [Lat] (eks GRAY-shuh) A payment made as a favour, not by legal right.

ex libris [Lat] From the library of. Usually seen on bookplates.

ex nihilo nihil fit [Lat] Nothing produces nothing.

ex officio [Lat] By virtue of one's office.

ex ore parvulorum veritas [Lat] Out of the mouths of babes comes truth.

ex parte [Lat] (eks PART-ay) In law, in the interests of one party only; a temporary injunction granted to one party in the absence of the other.

ex post facto [Lat] After the deed; becoming effective retrospectively.

extrait [Fr] A copy of a certificate; an extract: *extrait de naissance* – birth certificate; *extrait mortuaire* – death certificate.

extraordinaire [Fr] Extraordinary; exceptional.

ex voto [Lat] Something done in accordance with a vow; a votive object.

F

fabbrica [It] A factory.

faber est quisque fortunae suae [Lat] We are all architects of our fortunes.

façade d'honneur [Fr] The main frontage of a building.

facile largire de alieno [Lat] It is easy to be generous with what is another's.

facile princeps [Lat] (fa-see-lay PRIN-seps) Easily the best; the acknowledged leader.

façon de parler [Fr] Way of speaking; mere words, all effect and no sincerity.

facta non verba [Lat] Deeds, not words.

factotum [Lat] A jack-of-all-trades.

fac ut gaudeam [Lat] Make my day.

fadastikos! [Gk] Fantastic!

fahrt [Ger] Ubiquitous word important to car drivers: *Durchfahrt verboten* – No entry; *Ausfahrt* – Exit; *Einfahrt frei halten* – Do not block entrance, etc.

faire la sourde oreille [Fr] To turn a deaf ear.

faire ses choux gras [Fr] To fatten your cabbages; to feather your nest.

fait accompli [Fr] An accomplished fact; something already done.

faits divers [Fr] Short news items; news in brief.

faites vos jeux [Fr] (fet voh ZHUR) Place your bets.

falafel [Arab] Fried chickpeas sometimes served in pitta bread.

False friends

They're called *Faux Amis,* dangerous duos, treacherous twins, *Mots-Pièges,* false friends. And with good reason: they are words of a foreign language that so closely resemble English words that we assume they share the same meaning. On the contrary: many have completely different meanings, and howlers inevitably result when the user is unaware of the difference. Here is just a small selection:

French false friends

Agenda: notebook, diary. *Commodité:* comfort, convenience. *Délayer:* to dilute, water down. *Demander:* sometimes to demand but also a mild request. *Éventuel:* possible. *Lunatique:* capricious, fickle. *Pet:* fart. *Prétendre:* to assert, to claim. *Supplier:* to beseech. *User:* to wear out.

German false friends

Bald: soon. *Chef:* boss, manager. *Fast:* almost, nearly. *Fatal:* annoying. *Fix:* quick, smart. *Genial:* brilliant, gifted, brainy. *Kaution:* guarantee, deposit. *Gift:* poison. *Slip:* knickers. *Spenden:* to give, to donate.

Italian false friends

Accidenti: damn! *Camera:* room. *Confetti:* sugar-coated almonds. *Lunatico:* moody. *Magazzino:* storehouse. *Parente:* a relation. *Promiscuo:* mixed. *Rumore:* noise. *Sofisticato:* adulterated. *Suggestivo:* striking, picturesque. *Superbo:* arrogant.

Spanish false friends

Advertir: to give warning. *Carpeta:* office file. *Constipado:* suffering from a cold. *Extenuar:* to weaken. *Injuria:* insult.

INTOXICADO: NOT DRUNK BUT POISONED

Intoxicado: not drunk but poisoned. *Particular:* private, personal. *Suceso:* an event, happening. *Tormenta:* storm. *Voluble:* changeable.

---

farce est jouée [Fr] 'The comedy is over' – see *tirez le rideau.*

farceur [Fr] (far-SUR) A wag or practical joker; a writer of stage farce.

farouche [Fr] (fah-ROOSH) Shy or sullen.

fasullo [It] False, fake.

fata morgana [It] (far-tuh mor-GA-nuh) Originally a mirage seen in the Straits of Messina; now any mirage or similar illusion.

faubourg [Fr] (foh-boorg) An inner suburb, usually a

working-class neighbourhood.

fausse dévote [Fr] Pious hypocrite.

faute de mieux [Fr] (foht duh MYUR) For want of something better.

fauteuil [Fr] (foh-TIE) An armchair with sides that are not upholstered.

faux bonhomme [Fr] (foh bon-OM) Seemingly friendly and generous, but in fact not.

faux frais [Fr] Incidentals, details.

faux ménage [Fr] An ill-matched married couple.

faux naif [Fr] (foh nah-EEF) Pretending to be sincere and honest.

faux pas [Fr] (foh pah) An indiscretion; a mistake; a social slip one regrets.

favela [Port] A shantytown in Brazil.

fecit [Lat] (FEH-kit) He/she made it. Seen on older paintings, sculpture, medals, coins, etc.

fee sehatak [Arab] Cheers!

fellah [Arab] In Arabic countries, a peasant.

felo de se [Lat] Literally, felon of yourself. Someone who commits suicide.

femme de chambre [Fr] (fam duh SHARM-bruh) Chambermaid.

femme fatale [Fr] (fam fat-AHL) A seductress who brings woe and ruination to her lovers.

femme savante [Fr] Bluestocking.

feng shui [Ch] (feng SHOO-ee, fung shway) Chinese method of laying out a home or workplace to maximize the harmony of spiritual energy.

fermatevi [It] Stop!

fermeture annuelle [Fr] ('annual closing') The French summer holiday period in August when a good part of Paris shuts down and huge numbers of Parisians leave the city.

Ferry crossing

Amusing cross-fertilisations of English and French are not unknown on the cross-channel ferries. One fairly common loudspeaker announcement is, first in English: 'Ladies and gentlemen, the *buffet* is now open.' This is followed by the translation: *'Mesdames et messieurs, le* **snack bar** *est ouvert maintenant.'*

Ferragosto [It] The Italian bank holiday on August 15.

festina lente [Lat] Hasten slowly; more haste, less speed.

festschrift [Ger] Collection of essays or other writings made in honour of someone.

fête champêtre [Fr] An outdoor or country festival.

fête nationale [Fr] A country's national day, such as July 14, Bastille Day.

feu de joie [Fr] (fur duh ZHWAR) A sustained salute by rifle fire at public ceremonies.

feuilleton [Fr] A serialised novel; that part of a newspaper devoted to fiction or light reading.

fianchetto [It] In chess, the flank development of a bishop to control a key diagonal.

fiat Dei voluntas [Lat] God's will be done.

flat lux [Lat] Let there be light.

Fidei Defensor [Lat] (fee-day-ee def-EN-sor) Defender of the Faith. The abbreviation **Fid Def** or **FD** can be seen on certain British coins.

fidus Achates [Lat] A faithful friend; an intimate companion.

filer à l'anglaise [Fr] Surreptitiously to slip away; to take 'French leave'.

fille de joie [Fr] A courtesan; prostitute.

fille du regiment [Fr] An army prostitute.

film noir [Fr] The genre of moody, cynical crime films made in Hollywood in the 1940s and 1950s.

fils [Fr] Son. Used after the surname to distinguish the son from the father, eg 'Jones fils'.

fin de siècle [Fr] (fa(n) duh SYEK-luh) End of the century, specifically the end of the nineteenth century, with the suggestion of decadence and aestheticism.

fines herbes [Fr] (feen ZERB) Mixed chopped herbs.

finis coronat opus [Lat] The end crowns the work.

finita la commedia [It] The comedy is over; the farce has ended.

fin sourire [Fr] A knowing smile.

flambé [Fr] Set alight. In cooking, to soak with brandy and ignite just before serving.

flâneur [Fr] (fla-NUR) A loafer; idle man-about-town.

flecti, non frangi [Lat] To be bent, not broken.

fleur-de-lis [Fr] (fluhr duh LEES) Heraldic flower in the royal arms of France..

flic [Fr] Cop; slang term for a police officer.

floreat [Lat] (FLOH-ree-at) May (it) flourish. The motto of Eton College: *floreat Etona*.

floruit; fl. [Lat] He/she flourished. Used to state the period in which someone in history was most active when the actual birth/death dates are not known.

folâtre [Fr] Playful.

folie [Fr] (fol-ee) Madness; delusions.

folie à deux [Fr] Madness or delusions simultaneously affecting two people who are close.

folie de grandeur [Fr] (fol-ee duh grah(n)-DUR) Delusions of grandeur; illusions of greatness.

fondre en larmes [Fr] To burst into tears; literally, 'to melt into tears'.

Football French

Staging, and above all winning, the 1998 Football World

Cup tournament certainly propelled France to the forefront of the game. Monoglot British fans who ventured over the Channel for the first time had, if nothing else, a wonderful opportunity to widen their outlook by exposure to the French twist on the vocabulary of the game they call *le foot*. Here are a few French equivalents of the expressions that are so dear to players, fans and commentators alike:

je suis aux anges	I'm over the moon
c'est à dégueuler	I'm sick as a parrot
à la mi-temps, ce n'est pas fini	It's a game of two halves
T'es aveugle, ou quoi?	Are you blind, ref?
on s'est fait arnaqué	We wuz robbed!
quelle passoire ce gardien de but	That keeper's useless
allons prendre un pot	Let's go for a pint

force de frappe [Fr] A strike force; now used to mean a nuclear deterrent.

force majeure [Fr] (fors ma-ZHUR) A superior, irresistible force; a compelling circumstance that will release a party (e.g. an insurance company) from fulfilling a contract.

foulard [Fr] Headscarf or neckerchief.

fou qui se tait passe pour sage [Fr] A fool who holds his tongue passes for a wise man.

fous-moi le camp/foutez-moi le camp [Fr] Bugger off! (A French stickler for propriety would insist on the latter form being used for someone one doesn't know well.)

fraise [Fr] Strawberry *Fraises des bois* – wild strawberries.

framboise [Fr] Raspberry.

Fighting off *franglais*

The French effort to safeguard the purity of their language and to resist the nasty infection known as *franglais* is fairly well known. To their credit, the French care far more about their language than do users of English; we tend to welcome just about any new word from anywhere, cheerfully tolerate any novel usage and avert our gaze from serious word abuse.

The French, however, are proudly protective of their precise and elegant language. During the 1980s hundreds of foreign words were banned and Académic française invented French words to replace them. *Animateur* replaced disc jockey; *navire-citerne* replaced tanker; *remue-meninges* replaced brainstorming; *ordinateur* replaced computer. The French also won the battle to name Concord *Concorde* and insisted that in France a jet was *avion à réaction.*

Linguistic transgressors were hauled before the courts. TWA was fined for using English-language boarding passes at Charles de Gaulle Airport. Evian, the bottled water company, was fined for calling its new product '*le* fast drink *des Alpes*'. The Paris Opera was sued for selling English-language programmes for the stage hit *Bubbling Brown Sugar.* A furniture maker was sued by Agulf (Association of Users of the French Language) for using the term 'showroom' instead of *salle d'exposition.*

But have the prohibitors succeeded? It appears not, for whatever officialdom may have decreed, French youth went its own freewheeling way, gobbling up western words from rock and pop albums and from the fashion, sporting, computer and business worlds. By the end of 1992 the venerable Académie française, the official arbiters of the language, bowed to partial defeat as it admitted 5,900 new words to the Gallic lexicon. Overnight, *le* **bestseller,** *le* **bluejean,** *le* **clergyman,** *le* **cowboy,** *le* **dancing** and hundreds of other English words became officially French. Many others were accepted with the thinnest of veneers: bulldozer became *bouldozeur*; handshake became *shake-hand* and walkie-talkie became *talkie-walkie*. The surrender was, observed one academician, the only way to *solutionner un problème*.

However, the battle with *franglais* is not yet over. Language cleansing goes on, with laws threatening fines and even jail sentences for using foreign words in newspapers, advertising and official documents. Perhaps the French authorities should contemplate a French phrase that's long been a favourite *bon mot* in English: *c'est la vie.*

---

frappé [Fr] (frah-pay) Chilled and iced; liqueur poured over crushed ice.

frapper [Fr] To strike; to knock. *Entrez sans frapper* – enter without knocking.

Frau [Ger] (frow) Married woman; equivalent to Mrs.

Fräulein [Ger] (FROY-leyn) Formerly unmarried woman; now equivalent to Ms.

fraus est celare fraudem [Lat] It is fraud to conceal a fraud.

frère [Fr] (frair) Brother.

fresser [Yidd] Glutton.

freundlich [Ger] Kind, friendly, genial.

fricassée [Fr] Stewed meat and vegetables served with a sauce.

fricatrice [Fr] Lesbian; female homosexual.

frijoles [Sp] (frih-HOLE-ays) Widely cultivated Mexican beans.

frisch auf! [Ger] Cheer up!

fritto misto [It] (free-toh mees-toh) Dish of mixed fried seafood.

Fröhliche Weihnachten! [Ger] Merry Christmas!

froideur [Fr] (frwar-dur) Cooling; a romantic relationship that is cooling off.

froides mains, chaud amour [Fr] Cold hands, warm love (heart).

fronti nulla fides [Lat] There's no trusting to appearances.

frou-frou [Fr] (froo-froo) Originally the rustle of a woman's skirts; now over-frilly, fussy ornamentation.

frühe Hochzeit, lange Liebe [Ger] Early marriage, long love.

fruits de mer [Fr] (frwee duh MAIR) Sea-food.

frustra laborat qui omnibus placere studet [Lat] He labours in vain who attempts to please everyone.

Fulano, Mengano y Zutano [Sp] The Spanish equivalent of 'Tom, Dick and Harry'. *Fulano* is used for 'So-and-so' when referring to someone whose name you can't remember.

Funkstreife [Ger] Police radio patrol.

furor scribendi [Lat] A passion for writing.

Fürst der Schatten [Ger] The Prince of Shades: death.

fustanella [It] The stiff white cotton dress worn by Greek soldiers during ceremonial occasions.

futsch [Ger] Done for; had it: ***der Wagen ist futsch*** – the car has had it.

G

gaieté de cœur [Fr] Light-heartedness.

galette [Fr] The round, flat cake made to celebrate Twelfth Night on January 6. *Galette* is also slang for money.

gamine (fem); **gamin** (masc) [Fr] (gah-MEEN; gah-MAH(N)) Having the impudence of a street urchin.

ganar [Sp] (gah-NAR) To make or win money.

gant de toilette [Fr] Wash cloth, the equivalent of the English flannel, although often a towelling glove.

garce [Fr] Slang for 'bitch'.

garçon [Fr] (GAR-sor(n)) Waiter; boy.

Garda [Ir] A police officer, or the Irish police force, in full *Garda Síochána* (Guard of the Peace).

gardez bien [Fr] Take good care.

gare [Fr] Railway station; platform. *Chef de gare* – station master; *Gare du Nord* – Northern Paris terminal.

gare! [Fr] Look out!

Gastarbeiter [Ger] (GAST-ar-byter) Literally, guest worker. An immigrant worker.

Gasthaus [Ger] Small inn or restaurant in Germany.

Gasthof [Fr] Hotel or inn in Germany.

gauche [Fr] (gohsh) Clumsy; socially inept.

gaudeamus igitur [Lat] (gow-day-AHM-us IG-ee-tur) Let us therefore rejoice! First line of the well-known students' drinking song.

gavroche [Fr] Street arab, from the gamin Gavroche in
Hugo's *Les Misérables*.

gazpacho [Sp] Cold tomato and cucumber soup,
a speciality of Andalusia.

gefilte (fish) [Yidd] Balls of seasoned minced fish cooked
in broth.

gemütlich [Ger] (guh-MOOT-likh) Good-natured, kindly.

genius loci [Lat] Literally, spirit of the place. The
characteristic atmosphere of a particular place.

gens de bien [Fr] Respectable folk.

gens de couleur [Fr] People of colour.

German

German is spoken by more than 100 million people and is
the official language of Germany and Austria and a
principal language of Switzerland. Of the two main varieties
Plattdeutsch (Low German) and *Hochdeutsch* (High
German), the Low variety has a strong affinity with
English. If you visit Schleswig-Holstein or anywhere along
the north German coast, you will hear people saying they
were born in 'neinteyn-hunder-fife-und-dirtig' (1935),
talking about the 'veather' being 'colt' and asking 'what ist
duh klok?' You are, of course, in that part of Germany from
which in the fifth century the Angles decided to move to
what is now England, along with the Saxons and the Jutes.
That is perhaps why, apart from the difficult grammar and
the propensity for word-building (something as simple as a
matchbox is called a *Steichholzschachtelchen*), the English
have little difficulty with German pronunciation. Almost
automatically we sense that

au is pronounced as *ow* as in *Frau*
ei is pronounced as *eye* as in *Heine*
ie is pronounced as *ee* as in *diesel*
ee is pronounced as *ay* as in *Beethoven*

ch is pronounced as *kh* as in **Bach**
j is pronounced as *y* as in **Jaeger**
w is pronounced as *v* as in **Wagner**
z is pronounced as *ts* as in **Mozart**

The Germans are not so protective as the French about their language (although the **Deutscher Sprachverein**, the German Language Society, sniffs out transgressions and, to quote one example, insists that the wrestling hold called the hammerlock should be called **Ellenbogengelenkschlüssel**) and unsurprisingly it is becoming littered with anglicisms: **Pressekonferenzen, no komment, off die rekord, der Teenager, das Walkout, ein Steadyseller, der Cashflow** are some random (and horrible) examples.

---

gesacht, getan [Ger] No sooner said than done.

Gesämtkunstwerk [Ger] A total work of art; a combination of different forms of art in one work, such as music, drama, and poetry combining to make up an opera.

Gesellschaft [Ger] Company; association; society.

Gesellschafterin [Ger] Call-girl; hired female escort.

Gesetz ist mächtig, mächtiger ist die Not [Ger] The law is mighty but necessity is mightier (Goethe).

Gesundheit! [Ger] (guh-ZOONTH-hyt) Good health! Said to someone who sneezes; also used as a toast.

> **Gesundheit is besser als Reichtum –** health is better than riches.

geteilte Freude ist doppelte Freude [Ger] A joy shared is a joy doubled.

gettane le margherite ai porci [Ger] To throw pearls before swine.

Gewerkschaft [Ger] Trade union.

gigot [Fr] (zhee-goh) Leg of mutton.

gillie; ghillie [Gael] A helper or guide in the Scottish

Highlands hunting regions.

giri [Jap] To observe one's moral duty in society.

gitano [Sp] Gypsy.

gîte [Fr] (zheet) A furnished holiday cottage or small house for let in rural France.

glacé [Fr] (glahs-say) Glazed; iced with sugar.

Glasgow German

When it was discovered that four Germans in the dock of a Glasgow court could speak no English, a man in the public gallery promptly offered to interpret, saying that he had learned the language as a prisoner of war.

The Sheriff then addressed the first German: 'What is your name?' (*Wie heißen Sie?*)

The interpreter translated: 'Vot iss your name, hein?' He was charged with contempt of court.

---

glasnost [Rus] (GLAS-nuhst) Literally, publicity. Openness; receptiveness to criticism.

gloire [Fr] (glwahr) French patriotic sense of honour and glory.

gloria in excelsis Deo [Lat] Glory be to God on high. The prayer that follows the Kyrie of the Mass.

Glück auf! Glück zu! [Ger] Good luck! *Glück auf den Weg* – have a pleasant journey.

Gluhwein [Ger] Mulled wine, often indulged in *après-ski*.

gnocchi [It] (NYOK-ee) Dumplings, served with soup or sauce.

gombeen-man [Ir] Money-lender.

Gongchandang [Ch] Communist Party.
   Gongchandangyuan – Party member.

gospodart [Rus] Gentleman.

Gospodin [Rus] Master. The equivalent to Mr or Sir.

Götterdämmerung [Ger] (gur-tuh-DEM-uh-rung) The twilight of the Gods; the end of the world.

Gott mit uns [Ger] God with us; motto of the Prussian
kings.

Gott sei dank [Ger] God be thanked.

gouine [Fr] Crude term for a lesbian; female homosexual.

goûter [Fr] Literally, to taste. A kind of French afternoon
tea or snack, indulged in at about 4 p.m.

gracias a Dios [Sp] Thanks to God.

gradatum vincimus [Lat] We conquer step by step.

graffito [It] A slogan, often indecent, painted or scratched
on walls. The form most used is the plural, *graffiti*.

GRAFFITO

grande amoureuse [Fr] (grah(n)d am-uh-rurz) A woman
who gives her life to love affairs.

grande dame [Fr] (grah(n)d dam) Great lady; aristocratic.

grande école [Fr] (grah(n)d ay-KOL) One of a number of prestigious French Colleges of higher education of which the military *École Polytechnique* is the best known.

grande passion [Fr] A passionate and serious love affair.

grande vedette [Fr] A famous film or stage star.

Grand Guignol [Fr] (grah(n) GEE-nyol) A short, macabre play intended to horrify.

grand mal [Fr] (grah(n) mal) Violent form of epilepsy.

grand siècle [Fr] The seventeenth century; the age of Louis XIV.

gran turismo [It] High-performance touring car.

grappa [It] Italian brandy made from grape pressings.

gratia gratiam parit [Lat] Kindness produces kindness.

gravadlax; gravlax [Swed] Dry-cured spiced salmon.

   Gravad strömming – dry-cured spiced herring.

graviora manent [Lat] The worst is yet to come.

Is it all Greek to you?

Greek can be frustrating. The spoken language comes in a variety of local dialects as well as, a classical version (***Katharevusa***) and the popular speech (***Demotic***) which is now the official state language.

Written Greek, at least when written in capital letters, looks accessible because much of the alphabet appears to resemble our own: A is **alpha,** B is **beta,** K is **kappa,** M is **mu** and so on. But it departs somewhere with letters which have no English equivalents: ψ or **psi** (pronounced **ps** as in **lapse**), X or **chi** (pronounced **ch** as in **loch**) and θ or **theta** (pronounced **th** as in **thought**).

Here's a little quiz to tweak your Greek. Make six common words from the fragments below by inserting the names of Greek letters. *(Answers on page 170)*

1. *m - - - llic*	4. *ca - - - ze*
2. *ca - - - p*	5. *ma - - - nery*
3. *- - - losophy*	6. *res - - - rant*

gringo [Sp] Literally, foreigner. A disparaging term in Latin America for an English speaker or North American (actually means different things in different countries).

grisette [Fr] Literally, grey dress fabric. A young working-class woman.

Groschenroman [Ger] The equivalent of English 'penny dreadful' novels, bodice-rippers and wild west pulp novels.

gros mot [Fr] Colloquial for swearword.

guasto [It] Out of order.

guberniya [Rus] Administrative division of the former Soviet Union.

gueule de bois [Fr] Literally, wooden face (or jaws). A colloquial term for a hangover.

guerre à outrance [Fr] Total warfare; duel to the death.

Gum [Rus] (goom) State Universal Shop: the large Moscow department store.

gute Besserung [Ger] A wish for a speedy recovery.

Gymnasium [Ger] Grammar school. Pupils are 11-16 years but most stay for a further three years.

H

habeas corpus [Lat] Literally, you may have the body. A writ ordering a person to appear before the court to establish whether or not detention is lawful.

habitué [Fr] A regular customer.

habrit ha khadasha [Heb] The New Testament.

haciendado [Sp] A person owning property; proprietor of a *hacienda*.

hachimaki [Jap] The ubiquitous headbands worn by males to encourage concentration and effort.

hadj; hajj [Arab] The Muslim pilgrimage to Mecca.

hadji; hajji [Arab] A Muslim who has made the pilgrimage to Mecca.

haec olim meminisse juvabit [Lat] In time it will be pleasing to remember (these events).

haiku [Jap] (hy-koo) Japanese poem of just three lines and a total of seventeen syllables arranged 5, 7, 5.

haka [Mao] (HAH-kuh) Maori war dance made familiar by the All Blacks rugby team before their games.

Hakenkreuz [Ger] Literally, hooked cross. The swastika.

hakuna matata [Swa] No worries!

halal [Arab] Meat from animals slaughtered according to Muslim law.

halászlé [Hung] Thick paprika-flavoured fish soup.

Halbstarker [Ger] A teenage hooligan; a delinquent.

hapax legomenon [Gk] A word or saying unique in any written language; used only once.

hara-kiri [Jap] Literally, guts slit. Samurai suicide by disembowelling.

hare Krishna [Sans] Hail to Krishna.

hashi [Jap] Chopsticks.

hasta la muerte todo es vida [Sp] Until death, all is life; while there's life there's hope.

hasta la vista [Sp] Goodbye; until we meet again.

haud fiet, et clavo fixum est [Lat] Nothing doing, and that's final!

Haus und Hof [Ger] House and home.

Hausfrau [Ger] (hows frow) German housewife – not generally complimentary.

haute bourgeoisie [Fr] (oht boor-zhwah-zee) The upper-middle or professional class.

haute couture [Fr] (oht kuh-TUUR) High fashion dress design.

haute cuisine [Fr] (oht kwih-ZEEN) Top class cooking.

haute école [Fr] (oht EKOLL) Classical art of horse-riding.

haut monde [Fr] (oh mond) High society.

heb' dich weg von mir, Satan [Ger] Get thee behind me, Satan.

Heimat [Ger] Home; one's birthplace.

Heimweh [Ger] Homesickness.

hendiadys [Lat via Gk] A figure of speech in which two nouns are linked by a conjunction for effect: **fear and loathing, gloom and despondency**, etc., instead of **fearful loathing, gloomy despondency**.

Herrenvolk [Ger] Master race: Nazi term for the German people.

Herzchen [Ger] Darling.

heute mir, morgen dir [Ger] My turn today, yours tomorrow.

hic et ubique [Lat] Here and everywhere.

hic jacet [Lat] (heek YAK-et) Here lies (followed by name of deceased).

Himmel [Ger] Heavens!

hinc illae lacrymae [Lat] Literally, hence those tears. That's the cause.

hin ist hin [Ger] Gone is gone; forget it.

Hinz und Kunz [Ger] The equivalent of 'Tom, Dick and Harry'; sometimes *Krethi und Plethi*.

hiraeth [Welsh] (HEER-ayth) A mingled feeling of sadness, somewhere between homesickness and nostalgia.

hoch soll er leben [Ger] Long may he live.

hoi polloi [Gk] (hoy puh-LOY) The masses; the common multitude. Pedantically correct without 'the', but usage now accepts *the hoi polloi*.

¡hola! [Sp] Greeting to friends, roughly equivalent to 'hullo'.

homard [Fr] (om-mahr) Lobster.

homme d'affaires [Fr] (om dah-FARE) A businessman.

homme de lettres [Fr] (om duh let-ruh) Man of letters.

homme du monde [Fr] (om doo MO(N)D) A man of the world.

Homo sapiens [Lat] Literally, wise man. The name given to modern man as a species.

homo trium literatum [Lat] A thief. The phrase translates as 'three letter man' meaning *fur*, Latin for thief.

honi soit qui mal y pense [Fr] Shame on him who thinks ill of it. Motto of the Order of the Garter.

hora fugit [Lat] The hour flies.

horresco referens [Lat] I shudder to tell.

horribile dictu [Lat] (ho-REEB-ee-lay dik-too) Horrible to tell. The opposite is *mirabile dictu* – wonderful to tell.

hors concours [Fr] (or koh(n)-koor) Superior, therefore not in competition; not competing for any prize.

hors de combat [Fr] (or duh koh(n)-bah) Out of the fight; disabled.

hors d'œuvre [Fr] (or DURV) Appetiser before main
course.

hortus siccus [Lat] Literally, dry garden. A herbarium;
collection of dried plants.

hôtel des postes [Fr] General post office.

hôtel de ville [Fr] Town hall.

hoteru [Jap] Hotel.

hubris [Gk] Excessive pride or arrogance, especially of the
kind that leads to someone's downfall.

huîtres [Fr] (WEET-ruh) Oysters.

Hungarian

One of the first things you notice about Hungarian is the
density of the diacritics, including loads of umlauts and
acres of acute accents. **Thank you** is rendered as *köszönöm
szépen*; **spa** is *gyógyfürdöhely*. The chief reason for all these
marks is that every vowel forms a syllable and all vowels
are pronounced separately, even where several follow each
other. Until you master the system you might as well be
talking to a Tibetan. Forms of address are important in
Hungary, too. There are three words for **you**: *te,* which is
used when addressing family and children; the everyday
maga, and the formal or polite *ön.* Confusing, yes; but not
as confusing as having to go to the *Stomatológiai Intézet* for
a dental emergency.

---

huzur [Arab] Your presence; polite form of address, as in
'Your Honour'.

hwyl [Welsh] (HOO-eel) Religious or emotional fervour, as
experienced with preaching, poetry reading, sporting
events, etc.

I

ibidem; ibid. [Lat] (IB-id-em) In the same place; used when referring to a quote previously cited.

IBID: THE NOISE MADE BY A FROG

ich danke Ihnen [Ger] I thank you.

ich dien [Ger] (ik DEEN) I serve. Motto of the Prince of Wales.

ich kann nicht anders [Ger] I can do no other. From a
speech by Martin Luther; now used in the sense of
standing by one's principles in the face of hostility.
ich liebe dich [Ger] (eek leeb-uh deek) I love you.
ici on parle français [Fr] French spoken here.
idée reçue [Fr] (eed-ay rih-soo) Received idea; something
that is generally accepted.
idem; id. [Lat] (id-dem) The same. To avoid repetition used
in footnotes to refer to an author already named.
id est; i.e. [Lat] That is; used to say something in other
words or explain what has been said.
iechyd da! [Welsh] Good health!
Iesus Nazarenus Rex Iudaeorum [Lat] Jesus of Nazareth,
King of the Jews. The initials ***INRI*** are often seen on
paintings of the Crucifixion.
i frutti proibiti sono I piu dolci [It] Forbidden fruits are
the sweetest.
ignis fatuus [Lat] Will-o'-the-wisp, a phosphorence seen in
swamps and marshes. Used now to mean a delusion or
a foolish idea.
Igiriss [Jap] Great Britain.
ikebana [Jap] The art of Japanese flower arranging.
ik hou van je [Dut] (eek how fan yuh) I love you.
il faut cultiver son jardin [Fr] We must cultivate our own
garden – Voltaire. We should attend to our own affairs.
il faut souffrir pour être belle [Fr] We (women) must
suffer to be beautiful.

Falling ill in France

The French have long been recognized as champion
hypochondriacs. Before the big summer break newpapers
run special supplements not on where to visit but on how
to deal with holiday diseases and ***le mal des transports*** –
travel sickness in all its rich variety: ***sensation de vertige***
(giddiness), ***état nauséeux*** (waves of nausea), ***sueurs***

abondants (profuse sweating), *accélération de rythme cardiaque* (erratic heartbeat) and *frissons* (shivering), not to mention *troubles digestifs avec vomissements* (stomach-ache with vomiting).

It is said that France is not a good country to get sick in. This is not to suggest that French medical care is in any way wanting; on the contrary, it is administered with morbid enthusiasm. The slightest sign of *constipation* – or, for that matter almost any malady and – you'll have a box of *suppositoires* slapped into your hand. And don't, whatever you do, *avoir une crise de foie*, which is to have a liver crisis or, less dramatically, *l'indigestion*. The French live and die by their livers and regard good health as a temporary aberration to normal living. So if you wish to avoid what may well be *le remède est pire que le mal* (the cure is worse than the illness), consider the alternative: *mieux vaut prévenir que guérir* (prevention is better than cure).

---

ils n'ont rien appris ni rien oublié [Fr] They have learned nothing and forgotten nothing. Said of the Court of Louis XVIII.

immer schlimmer [Ger] From bad to worse.

immobiliste [Fr] Someone who opposes change and progress.

imperméable [Fr] Raincoat.

imposta sul valore aggiunto [It] Known as *IVA* – the equivalent of Value Added Tax (VAT).

in absentia [Lat] In the absence (of the party concerned).

in alio loco [Lat] In another place.

inamorato [It] Lover. The feminine is *inamorata*.

in bona partem [Lat] (To be judged) favourably or sympathetically.

in camera [Lat] Conducted in private, rather than in an open court.

inconnu [Fr] Unknown; someone whose identity is not known.

Index Librorum Prohibitorum [Lat] For four centuries (1564-1966) the list of books prohibited or censored by the Roman Catholic Church.

India

Of the Indian sub-continent's billion plus people, India's population of over 900 million speak some 800 local languages, almost all of them mutually unintelligible. Obviously a lingua franca is vital for national communication and although English is not the only official language (Hindi has been since 1965) a version of it – Indian English – is spoken by tens of million and remains the language of culture, education and aspiration. English has absorbed many Indian words – **gymkhana, bungalow, copra, chintz, polo** and **pyjama** are just a few – and some millions of Britons who eat in Indian restaurants can claim familiarity with the names of a wide range of foods from the sub-continent – plus many invented in Britain!

in esse [Lat] In existence.

in extenso [Lat] At full length; entire.

in extremis [Lat] At the point of death.

in flagrante delicto [Lat] In the very act.

infra dignitatem; infra dig [Lat] Beneath one's dignity.

ingénue [Fr] An innocent, naive or unsophisticated young woman.

in hoc signo vinces [Lat] By this sign thou shall conquer.

in loco parentis [Lat] In the place of a parent; with the responsibilities and authority of parents.

in memoriam [Lat] In memory of (followed by name of deceased).

in nomine Patris et Filii et Spiritus Sancti [Lat] In the name of the Father, and of the Son, and of the Holy Spirit.

in perpetuum [Lat] For ever.

in puris naturalibus [Lat] (in pyoo-ris nat-yoo-RAHL-ih-bus) Starkers; naked.

in re [Lat] In the matter of; concerning.

in saecula saeculorum [Lat] For ever and ever; always.

insalutato hospite [Lat] Leaving without saying farewell to your host.

in situ [Lat] (in SIT-yoo) In its original place; undisturbed.

inter alia [Lat] Among other things.

interregnum [Lat] The period between reigns or rulers when the state is governed by a temporary authority.

in toto [Lat] Completely; entirely.

intoxicado [Sp] *Está intoxicado* means 'He is poisoned', not 'He is drunk'.

intoxication [Fr] Poisoning. *Intoxication alimentaire* – food poisoning. A notorious *faux ami (see article on False Friends, page 56)*.

intra vires [Lat] (in-truh VEE-reez) Within the power and authority of a person or institution.

in utero [Lat] In the womb.

in vino veritas [Lat] In wine there is truth; a drunk always speaks the truth.

in vitro [Lat] (in VEET-roh) In an artificial environment; in the laboratory.

in vivo [Lat] In the living organism; in the body.

ipse dixit [Lat] Literally, he himself said it. An unsupported assertion.

ipso facto [Lat] By that very fact.

is iyian [Gk] Cheers!

Italia para nacer, Francia para vivir, España para morir [Sp] Italy to be born in, France to live in, Spain to die in.

Italian

Most of us know enough about Italian to be aware that **c** before **e** or **i** is pronounced **ch** as in **church** and *ciao*; that **ch** is pronounced **k** as in *Chianti*; that the **g** of **gli** is silent as in *intaglio*; and that **z** and **zz** are pronounced **ts** as in *scherzo* and *intermezzo*. We know this because of the large number of Italian words that have been absorbed into English – especially in the fields of music, opera, food and drink – and because we continue to pronounce them the way the Italians do.

The Italians at home, however, find the going more complicated. Regional accents and dialects remain deep-rooted and millions of Italians have great difficulty in communicating with their fellow citizens. This is where the verbal gesture fills the gap, making the language one of the most expressive at football matches and in traffic arguments: *Bastardo! Stronzo! Maladetto fottuto!*

See also *polizia*.

Ivrit [Heb] Hebrew.
izvestia; izvestiya [Rus] Information; news. Also the title
of one of Russia's national newspapers.

J

j'accuse [Fr] Emile Zola's famous public letter in *l'Aurore* to the government of France in 1898, for which he risked all to tell all and which was headlined *J'Accuse!* has lent its name to any published accusation of injustice or intolerance.

alea jacta est [Lat] The die is cast; there is no turning back. Said to have been spoken by Julius Caesar when crossing the Rubicon.

j'adoube [Fr] Literally, I adjust. To be said during a chess game before touching a piece to adjust it rather than make a move.

jai alai [Basque] (hy-uh-ly) Ball game played with a small basket attached to a hand.

jalousie [Fr] (ZHAH-luh-zee) Slatted window shutters.

jamais de ma vie [Fr] Never in my life; emphatically never.

jamal [Arab] Camel.

jambon [Fr] Ham.

Japlish

Someone has estimated that since the end of World War II the Japanese have absorbed some 20,000 English words into their language – or approximately 10% of its lexicon. But when you look a little closer at this phenomenal appetite for words from the West you discover that in the process of digestion the English words have undergone a peculiar transformation. It has resulted in words that half-way resemble their English originals, and half-way sound like strangulated approximations of them. This new add-on to the Japanese language is called *Japlish*. Here are some examples:

erebeta	elevator	*bata*	butter
bifeteki	steak	*beisuboru*	baseball
Koka-Kora	Coca-Cola	*garafu*	golf
		huruts	fruit
remon	lemon	*bijinesuman*	businessman
omuret	omelette		

Some words, like *no-pan,* look and sound convincingly Japanese until you are told that it means bottomless waitress.

There exists, however, a world outside *Japlish*, where there is an increasing tendency amongst Japanese to use English words and phrases in contexts that are utterly meaningless. Try these:

- *Too old to die, too young to happy* – slogan on a cream soda.

- *Green piles* – brand of lawn fertiliser.

- *Pocket Wetty* – premoistened towelettes.

- *Fingernail Remover* – fingernail cleaner.

- *Hand-Maid Queer-Aid* – brand of chocolate bar.

- *Poccari Sweat* and *Homo Milk* – popular soft drinks.

- *Nazal – for stuffed nose and snot* – on nasal spray pack.

jardin des plantes [Fr] Botanical garden.

jawohl [Ger] (yah-vohl) Yes, certainly.

Jehad; Jihad [Arab] A crusade inspired by strongly-held beliefs; specifically a Muslim holy war against unbelievers and enemies of Islam.

jellaba; djellabah [Arab] The loose-hooded cloak worn by males in some Arab countries.

je m'en fous [Fr] I don't give a damn.

je ne regrette rien [Fr] I regret nothing.

je ne sais quoi [Fr] I don't know what. Something that one can't specify or define.

jenever [Dut] Dutch gin.

je t'aime [Fr] (zh tem) I love you.

jeu de mots [Fr] (zhur duh moh) A play on words; for example, a pun.

jeu d'esprit [Fr] (zhur de-spree) A lighthearted witticism or display of cleverness.

jeune fille [Fr] (zhurn fee-yuh) Young girl.

jeunesse dorée [Fr] (zhurn-ess dor-ray) Gilded youth. The wealthy and fashionable young.

jiàngyóu [Ch] Soy sauce.

joie de vivre [Fr] (zhwah duh veev-ruh) Joy of life; high spirits.

jolie laide [Fr] A woman whose lack of beauty or irregular features are in themselves attractive or charming. Also called: *belle laide*.

jour de fête [Fr] (zhoor duh fet) A feast day.

Judenhetze [Ger] Anti-Semitism.

ju-jitsu; jiu-jitsu [Jap] Japanese style of wrestling, using the opponent's strength to unbalance and throw them. *Judo* is a refinement of *ju-jitsu*.

julienne [Fr] Shredded vegetables, often made into soup by adding to meat broth.

junta [Sp] (JUHN-tuh in UK; HOON-tah in Spanish) An

unelected group, usually military officers, holding power.

jure divino [Lat] By divine right.

jus [Fr] (zhoo) A sauce in which a dish is served.

juste milieu [Fr] (zhoost meel-yur) The happy medium; the golden mean; a middle course.

justification du tirage [Fr] Proof of the number of copies printed of limited edition books and prints.

j'y suis, j'y reste [Fr] (zhee swee, zhee rest) Here I am, here I stay.

K

kabuki [Jap] Popular drama in Japan.

kafenio [Gk] Coffee-house.

Kaffeeklatsch [Ger] (KAF-ay-klatsh) The gossip of a group (usually women) having coffee. Often mistakenly used to mean a 'coffee morning'.

kakemono [Jap] Japanese hanging scroll picture on rollers.

kalamarakia [Gk] Fried squid.

kalashnikov [Rus] A semiautomatic assault rifle.

Kamerad [Ger] Comrade! Its use dates from World War I and was the cry of surrendering German soldiers.

Kampf der Anschauen [Ger] A conflict of opinions.

Kamooneesteechyeskaya parteeya [Rus] Communist Party.

kan pei! [Ch] Bottoms up!; cheers!

Kapellmeister [Ger] (kah-PEL-meye-stuh) Orchestral or choir conductor.

kaput; kaputt [Ger] Done for; finished; had it.

karma [Sans] In Buddhism and Hinduism, the principle that a person's actions in the present life are responsible for that person's lot in a future reincarnation.

karaoke [Jap] Literally, empty orchestra. Amateur singing of well-known songs to a recorded backing track.

kashrut; kasher [Heb] Kosher.

Katzenjammer [Ger] Literally, the racket of mating cats. A monumental hangover.

KATZENJAMMER

Kaufhaus [Ger] Large department store.
kávé [Hun] Coffee.
Kazak [Rus] Cossack.
keiretsu [Jap] A corporate structure of interlinked businesses.

Keiner kann über sich sehn [Ger] No man can see
beyond himself. By this, the German philosopher
Schopenhauer meant that nobody can appreciate the
virtues of others without having some measure of those
virtues within themselves.

Kellner [Ger] Waiter; inn porter.

kermesse [Fr] A village fair or carnival. The Dutch version
is *kermis*.

khabar; khubber [Hindi] Information; a news report.

khidmatgar [Hindi] Waiter or table servant.

Khmer [Mon-Khmer] Official language of Cambodia,
spoken by about five million people.

khushi; khosh [Hindi; Pers] Happiness; pleasure; comfort;
to take one's pleasure. Via the Raj the English word
cushy derives from it.

kibbutz [Heb] Israeli collective farm or communal
industrial settlement. Plural: *kibbutzim*. *Kibbutznik* –
member of a *kibbutz*.

kibitzer [Yidd] Someone who interferes with unwanted
advice. *Kibitz* is the verb – to interfere.

kiblah [Arab] The direction (of Mecca) in which Muslims
pray.

kiquette, la; quéquette, la [Fr] Vulgar slang for penis.

Kinder, Kirche, Küche [Ger] Children, church, cooking – a
woman's lot in life.

kitsch [Ger] Anything vulgar or over-sentimental.

Kladderadatsch [Ger] A muddle; a mess.

Klappe [Ger] Mouth. *Halt die Klappe!* – shut up!

kleiner Mensch [Ger] Literally, small man. Narrow-
minded.

klutz [Yidd] Someone clumsy and stupid. Often used in
self-deprecation: 'I'm such a klutz!'

knäckebröd [Swed] Crispbread.

Knesset [Heb] The Israeli parliament.

Köchel [Ger] Usually abbreviated to *K*, the letter preceding the catalogue number of Mozart's compositions; thus K525 is his *Eine Kleine Nachtmusik*. From Ludwig von Köchel (1800-1877) who first classified the musician's works.

kotzen [Ger] Colloquial for vomiting; *es ist zum kotzen* – it's enough to make you sick.

krasi [Gk] Wine. *Krasi aspro* – white wine; *krasi kokino* – red wine.

Krasnaya Armeeya [Rus] Red Army.

Kraut [Ger] Uncomplimentary word for a German, from sauerkraut.

Kriminalroman; Krimi [Ger] Thriller novel.

Kripo [Ger] Colloquial shortening of *Kriminalpolizei*, the detective branch of the German police.

kukri [Hindi] Curved knife used by the Gurkhas.

Kümmel [Ger] Liqueur flavoured with caraway.

kung fu [Ch] Chinese martial art derived from karate and judo.

Kunst ist die rechte Hand der Natur [Ger] Art is the right hand of Nature (Schiller).

kwela [Xhosa, Zulu] Popular black music in South Africa, often featuring a penny whistle.

kvass [Rus] Russian beer made from grain and stale bread.

Kyrie; Kyrie eleison [Gk] Lord (have mercy). An invocation used in some Christian liturgies.

kyuji [Jap] Waiter.

L

la belle dame sans merci [Fr] Literally, the beautiful woman without mercy.

labore est orare [Lat] Work is prayer.

labore et honore [Lat] By labour and honour.

la critique est aisée et l'art est difficile [Fr] Criticism is easy and art is difficult.

lacrymae rerum [Fr] The tears of things; the sadness or tragedy of life.

ladna [Rus] Okay.

la donna è mobile [It] Woman is a fickle thing. The title of a song from Verdi's *Rigoletto*.

Leavings from the Lahore Hotel

Egg amlate, egg boil, corn flax, french toss, fry toss, butter toss, jam toss, fruit custed, cack custed, milk shik. Club sand whiches are Chicken Katlas. Snakes.

– from the menu of the Lahore Hotel, Khanewal, Pakistan

La Gioconda [It] The smiling lady. Another name for the Mona Lisa.

laissez-aller; laisser-aller [Fr] (less-ay ah-lay) Lack of constraint; letting things go; total freedom.

laissez-faire; laisser-faire [Fr] (less-ay fair) The policy of non-intervention, of not interfering, especially by a government.

lait [Fr] (lay) Milk. *au lait* – with milk.

La Manche [Fr] (lah mah(n)sh) The English Channel.

lambris d'appui [Fr] Wall panelling that rises to about a metre from the floor. *Lambris de hauteur* – floor-to-ceiling wall panelling.

Land [Ger] Country. *Länder* – German states. *Landtag* – legislature of a German state.

Landstraßenschreck [Ger] Colloquial: roadhog; rotten driver.

Langlauf [Ger] Cross-country or long-distance skiing.

langouste [Fr] Small spiny rock lobster.

langoustine [Fr] Small crayfish; large prawns.

lapin [Fr] Rabbit.

la propriété c'est le vol [Fr] Property is theft – Proudhon.

lapsus calami [Lat] (lap-sus KAL-uh-mee) A slip of the pen.

lapsus linguae [Lat] (lap-sus LING-way) Slip of the tongue.

lapsus memoriae [Lat] (lap-sus mem-OR-ee-ay) Slip of the memory.

larmes dans la voix [Fr] Literally, tears in the voice. The quaver in the voice that precedes tears.

l'art pour l'art [Fr] Art for art's sake, free of practical, social and moral restrictions.

lasciate ogni speranza voi ch'entrate [It] All hope abandon, ye who enter here: inscription over the gates of Hell from Dante's *Inferno*.

lass das Vergang'ne vergangen sein [Ger] Let bygones be bygones: from Goethe's *Faust*.

latet anguis in herba [Lat] There's a snake in the grass; something is concealed.

Latin

Latin is a dead tongue, as dead as dead can be,
First it killed the Romans; now it's killing me.
All are dead who wrote it,
All are dead who spoke it,
All are dead who learned it.
Lucky dead – they've earned it.

For a dead language, though, Latin is surprisingly persistent:
many of the English words we use in English **video,
propaganda** and **referendum** are derived from it, or still
survive intact – *post mortem, per annum, ad infinitum.* The
language arrived in Britain with the Romans, and had a
great revival in the Renaissance with the rediscovery of
classical texts. It was taken up by the church and the
medical and legal professions, by scholars and scientists of
all sorts, but is understood today only by a privileged few.

Latin has declined dramatically. It was abandoned as
the medium of Catholic worship in the 1960's under the
terms of the Second Vatican Council.

In the thirty years to 1992, the Queen's *annus
horribilis*, the number of students taking O-level Latin
shrank from 60,000 to under 14,000 – less than 2% of
children sitting GCSEs. Another ominous move was the
abandonment of Latin – for centuries used by doctors and
chemists to preserve their secrets – by the *British Medical
Journal.*

And yet, if you've browsed through some of the
hundreds of Latin entries in this book, you'll agree that it
possesses the economical and elegant knack of turning a
thought into an indelibly memorable phrase. Why, even
Waltzing Matilda has its Latin rendering:

Veni Matilda, veni Matilda,
Veni saltemus Matilda veni,
Et cantabat homo dum aestuaret cortina
Veni saltemus Matilda veni.

lato sensu [Lat] In the broad sense.

latte [It] Milk. *Latte condensato* – condensed milk; *latte detergente* – cleansing milk; *latte scremato* – skimmed milk.

lauda la moglie e tiente donzello [It] Praise a wife and married life but stay single.

lavabo [Lat] (lah-VAH-boh) Literally, I shall wash. The ritual washing of hands after offertory at Mass. In Italian and French, a washbasin or bathroom sink. In French a fairly common euphemism for the lavatory.

Lebensabend [Ger] The twilight of life.

leben Sie wohl! [Ger] Goodbye!

Lebensmut [Ger] Zest for life.

Lebensraum [Ger] Literally, living space. Territory claimed by a country for its expanding population. Especially applicable to Nazi Germany's annexation of border territory.

leben und leben lassen [Ger] Live and let live.

Leberwurst [Ger] Liver sausage.

le coût en ôte le goût [Fr] The cost spoils the taste.

leche [Sp] Milk, but *mala leche* is 'bad blood'.

la douceur de vivre [Fr] A gentle way of life.

le fin mot [Fr] The key point; the gist.

Légion d'honneur [Fr] (lay-zhor(n) doh-NUR) Legion of Honour, a civil or military order of merit introduced by Napoleon in 1802.

leitmotiv; leitmotif [Ger] Repeated theme, word, phrase, etc.

le meilleur vin a sa lie [Fr] Even the finest wine has dregs.

le monde [Fr] The world; mankind; society.

le mot de l'énigme [Fr] The key to the mystery.

le mot juste [Fr] The exact word; the perfect word for the purpose.

envoi [Fr] A postscript; a concluding verse or stanza.

le petit caporal [Fr] The little corporal: Napoleon.

le roi est mort; vive le roi [Fr] The king is dead; long live the king.

le Roi Soleil [Fr] The Sun King,: Louis XIV.

les cinq lettres [Fr] Four-letter words.

lèse-majesté [Fr] (layz-MAH-zhest-ay) High treason; an offence against the sovereign power of a state. In a watered-down sense, an attack on something sacrosanct.

les États-Unis [Fr] (layz aytahz-oo-nee) The United States (of America).

les petites gens [Fr] Humble people.

l'état, c'est moi [Fr] (lay-tah, say-mwar) I am the State. Attributed to Louis XIV.

le tout ensemble [Fr] Overall effect.

le vice anglais [Fr] (luh vees ah(n)-glay) Male homosexuality.

lex non scripta [Lat] Unwritten or common law.

lex talionis [Lat] Law of revenge; of retaliation.

Liar's Latin

One of the oldest games to be played with Latin is to invent new meanings to create sayings which look genuine but aren't. Here's a small collection to which you can add your own fabrications:

Sui generis: large serving of Chinese pork. *Hic jacet:* polyester sports coat. *De gustibus non est disputandum:* don't argue with the bus driver. *Reductio ad absurdum:* anorexia nervosa. *Et tu, Brute:* and two bottles of men's cologne, please. *Ex cathedra:* defrocked bishop. *Lapsus linguae:* lunch served on the Irish airline. *Summa cum laude:* God, it's hot! *Terra firma:* scared stiff. *ibid:* the noise made by a frog (see page 76). *Ad hoc:* this dish needs wine.

liberté, égalité, fraternité [Fr] Liberty, equality, fraternity. Motto of France.

libro cerrado no saca letrado [Sp] An unopened book never made a scholar.

licenciado [Sp] Licenciate; a university graduate.

licencié [Fr] A university graduate, but ***licencier*** means to give someone the sack.

Licht, Liebe, Leben [Ger] Light, love and life.

Liebchen [Ger] Darling! Beloved!

Liebeserklärung [Ger] A declaration of love.

Liebe wintert nicht [Ger] Love knows no winter.

Lieb und Leid [Ger] Joy and sorrow.

lied; lieder [Ger] (LEED-uh) German song, usually a solo with piano. The plural is ***lieder***.

limbus fatuorum [Lat] A fool's paradise.

lingua franca [It] A blend of Italian and other Mediterranean languages; nowadays any common language used by people with different mother tongues.

Literae Humaniores [Lat] Oxford degree subject concerned with Greek and Latin; the Classics.

litera scripta manet [Lat] The written word remains; it is always wise to put it in writing.

literati [Lat] Literary or scholarly people.

littérateur [Fr] (lih-teh-ruh-TUR) A writer; man of letters.

livre de chevet [Fr] A favourite book; a companion book.

locum tenens [Lat] Someone who replaces a professional colleague during an absence, especially doctors or dentists.

locus classicus [Lat] The authoritative statement on a subject.

loden [Ger] Green-grey woollen material used to make traditional Bavarian peasant clothing; now fashionable for all kinds of clothing.

l'œil du maître [Fr] The expert eye of the master.

logiciel [Fr] Computer software. It has been partly displaced by ***le software*** (*see article on Fighting off* franglais, page 62).

longueur [Fr] (lo(n)-GER) A long and tedious passage in a book, play, musical concert or speech.

lotteria [It] Lottery.

Lottoannahme [Ger] State lottery office.

louange perfide [Fr] Literally, treacherous praise. False praise intended to subvert and bring someone down.

lucri cause [Lat] For the sake of gain.

Lumpenproletariat [Ger] The disadvantaged, unambitious poor. Once commonly used in Marxist theory as a term of abuse, the word is now virtually defunct in left-wing political discourse.

l'union fait la force [Fr] Unity makes strength, motto of Belgium.

l'uomo propone, Dio dispone [It] Man proposes, God disposes.

lupus in fabula [Lat] Literally, the wolf in the fable. The unexpected appearance of someone just as he or she is being talked about.

lusus naturae [Lat] A freak of nature; one of nature's jokes.

lux et veritas [Lat] Light and truth.

lux mundi [Lat] Light of the world.

lycée [Fr] (LEE-say) One type of French secondary school.

M

maa as-salaamah [Arab] Goodbye.

ma biche [Fr] Literally, my doe. My darling.

macchabée [Fr] Corpse. Also colloquially **un macab**.

machismo; macho [Sp] Pride in masculinity.

Macht ist Recht [Ger] Might is right.

Machtpolitik [Ger] Power politics.

ma chère [Fr] (ma-shair) My dear (address only to women).

machin [Fr] Equivalent to English 'thingummy' or 'wotsit'.

Mädchen [Ger] Girl; maiden.

madeleine [Fr] Small sweet cake.

Hen Wlad fy Nhadau [Welsh] The land of my fathers: Welsh national anthem.

magari [Gk] If only it were so!

maggiore fretta, minore alto [It] More haste, less speed.

magister ceremoniarum; MC [Lat] Master of ceremonies

magna cum laude [Lat] (mag-nah kum-LOW-dih) With great distinction.

magna est veritas et praevalebit [Lat] Truth is great and shall prevail.

Magnificat [Lat] (mag-NIF-ih-kat) Hymn of the Virgin Mary: 'My soul doth magnify the Lord'; any hymn of praise.

magnum opus [Lat] Masterpiece; an artist's greatest work.

Magyarország [Hung] Hungary. A Hungarian is a *Magyar férfi* (man) or a *Magyar nö* (woman).

maharani [Hindi] A maharajah's wife or widow.

maharishi [Hindi] Hindu seer or wise man.

mahatma [Sans] Exponent of Buddhism; a sage.

Mahayana [Sans] A liberal branch of Buddhism.

maidan [Urdu] In India and Pakistan, a space for meetings or a sportsground.

maillot jaune [Fr] The yellow jersey worn by the points leader in the *Tour de France*.

mains froides, cœur chaud [Fr] Cold hands, warm heart.

mairie; maire [Fr] French town hall and mayor respectively.

maison de passe [Fr] A disreputable hotel, most likely a brothel. Such an establishment is also called a *maison de société* and a *maison de tolérance,* the latter being licensed.

maison de santé [Fr] Private hospital; nursing home.

maître d' [Fr] Hotel head-waiter.

maître de ballet; maîtresse de ballet [Fr] Person who trains and rehearses a ballet company.

maîtresse en titre [Fr] A man's recognized mistress.

makimono [Jap] Japanese scroll painting that unrolls horizontally.

maladresse [Fr] Clumsiness; lack of tact.

mal à propos [Fr] Literally, not to the purpose. Inappropriate. The word supplied Sheridan the inspiration for Mrs Malaprop for his play *The Rivals,* hence **malapropism:** the unintentional misuse of words with similar sounds.

mal d'amour [Fr] Love-sick.

mal de mer [Fr] (mal duh mair) Sea-sickness. Other *maux* include *mal du cœur* – nausea; *mal au ventre* – stomach ache; *mal de tête* – headache; *mal de dents* – toothache.

mal du siècle [Fr] World weariness; weariness of life.

male parte, male dilabuntur [Lat] Easy come, easy go.

malgré lui [Fr] (mal-gray LWEE) In spite of himself; against his will; contrary to his intentions.

malgré tout [Fr] (mal-gray TOO) In spite of everything.

malheur ne vient jamais seul [Fr] Troubles never come singly.

mal mariée An unhappily married woman.

Mamma mia! [It] My mother! An expression of surprise etc.

mammismo [It] Maternal control and interference by a mother that continues even when the family is fully grown.

mañana [Sp] Tomorrow. Sometime.

mancia [It] A tip or gratuity.

manga [Jap] Japanese style of comic books, often violent or graphically sexual in content

mano a mano [Sp] Hand-to-hand; one against one.

manqué [Fr] Unfulfilled; failed; would-be: 'Like most of his crowd he was just a writer *manqué*'.

manque de goût [Fr] Lack of good taste.

man spricht Deutsch [Ger] German spoken here.

maquerelle [Fr] The madam of a brothel.

maquillage [Fr] Cosmetics; make-up.

marché [Fr] Market. *Un marché decouvert* – an open-air market; *le Marché Commun* – (European) Common Market.

mare nostrum [Lat] 'Our sea': The Mediterranean.

mariage de convenance [Fr] (mar-ih-azh duh koh(n)-veh-nah(n)s) Marriage of convenience, usually with financial motive.

Marianne [Fr] Symbol of republican France and much prettier than John Bull or Uncle Sam.

marinare [It] To pickle; to marinate.

Mark Twain on the French language

'In Paris they simply stared when I spoke to them in French; I never did succeed in making those idiots understand their own language' . .

---

marmite [Fr] (mahr-MEET) Pot or saucepan.
marron glacé [Fr] Crystallized chestnut.
mashallah [Arab] God has willed it.
masjid; musjid [Arab] An Islamic mosque.
más vale tarde que nunca [Sp] Better late than never.
materfamilias [Lat] The mother or female head of the family.
matryoshka [Rus] Traditional Russian decorative dolls.

MATRYOSHKA DOLLS

matzo(h); matza(h) [Heb] Crisp unleavened bread eaten at Passover.
mauvais coucheur [Fr] (moh-vay koo-shur) Argumentative, cantankerous person.

mauvaise foi [Fr] (moh-vay fwah) Bad faith.

mauvais goût [Fr] (moh-vay goo) Bad taste.

mauvais moment [Fr] An unpleasant and embarrassing moment.

mauvais sang [Fr] Bad feeling; bad blood.

mauvais sujet [Fr] (moh-vay soo-zhay) A 'black sheep'.

maxima cum laude [Lat] With the highest praise and distinction.

maxima debetur puero reverentia [Lat] The greatest reverence is due to a child (Juvenal); a child should be protected from vulgarity and indecency.

maxime fabulosum [Lat] Absolutely fabulous!

mea culpa [Lat] The fault is mine; it's my fault.

médecine expectante [Fr] Nature's cure; medical treatment left to Nature.

medice, cure te ipsum [Lat] Physician, heal thyself.

meditatio fugae [Lat] Contemplating flight from justice.

Megali Vretania [Gk] Great Britain.

megillah [Yidd] An unnecessarily long and tiresome story or letter. From the Hebrew *Megillah*, the scroll of the Book of Esther.

Mehr Licht! [Ger] More light! Goethe's last words, 1832.

Mehrwertsteuer [Ger] Value added tax.

mein Gott! [Ger] My God!

Mein Kampf [Ger] *My Struggle*: Adolf Hitler's 1924 autobiography.

mélange [Fr] (may-lah(n)zh) A mixture; a confusion.

mêlée [Fr] (meh-lay) A confused affray; an unruly scramble.

melioribus annis [Lat] In happier times.

membrum virile [Lat] ('virile member') Penis.

memento mori [Lat] A reminder of death; a symbolic reminder of death (e.g. a skull).

ménage [Fr] (may-nahzh) A household; housekeeping.

ménage à trois [Fr] (may-nahzh ah TRWAH) A domestic

arrangement of husband and wife and a lover of one or both of them.

menefreghista [It] Like Rhett Butler, someone who doesn't give a damn.

mensch [Yidd] An admirable, honourable person.

mens rea [Lat] (mens ray-ah) With criminal intent; with the knowledge that an action is a criminal offence.

mens sana in corpore sano [Lat] A healthy mind in a healthy body.

menus plaisirs [Fr] For life's little pleasures; pocket money.

méprisable [Fr] Contemptible.

merci [Fr] (mair-see) Thank you.

merde [Fr] (maird) Excrement; shit. *Le merdier* – a mess.

meret qui laborat [Lat] He is deserving who is industrious.

mésalliance [Fr] (may-ZAL-ih-ah(n)s) A marriage with a partner who is socially inferior.

meschugge; meshugah [Yidd] Mad; silly; daft; crazy.

Messaggero [It] Messenger. The title of one of Italy's big national newspapers.

métèque [Fr] An alien; a foreigner.

métier [Fr] (may-tyay) A profession; something that someone is particularly good at doing.

métis [Fr] (may-tee) Someone of mixed blood (a term regarded as offensive by many). In Canada, of mixed American Indian and French-Canadian blood; in the US known as an octoroon.

metteur au point [Fr] Someone who provides the solution to a problem.

meum et tuum [Lat] (may-um et too-um) Mine and thine: the principle of the rights of property.

mezé [Turk] (mez-eh) Greek and near-Eastern appetizers served with drinks.

mi casa es su casa [Sp] My house is your house; make yourself at home.

miches [Fr] Vulgar slang in French for breasts.

Midi [Fr] The coastal plain contained by the Massif Central, Pyrenees and Alps in southern France.

midinette [Fr] Parisian shop assistant, usually in a dressmaker's or milliner's.

mierda [Sp] Spanish equivalent of *merde*.

mieux vaut tard que jamais [Fr] Better late than never.

mignon [Fr] (meen-yoh(n)) Small and dainty.

mijnheer [Dut] Dutch equivalent to 'Sir'.

Milchmädchenrechnung [Ger] Literally, milkmaid's reckoning. A conclusion or speculation based on faulty reasoning.

mille-feuilles [Fr] (meel FUR-yih) Iced puff pastry cakes filled with jam and cream.

millefiori [It] (mee-leh-FYOR-ih) Ornamental glassware which features flower patterns.

mille verisimili non fanno un vero [It] A thousand probabilities make not a single truth.

Minglish, or menus in mangled English

British travellers have for many years taken great delight in returning home with memories of distant cuisines expressed in a droll form of mangled English known as **Minglish**. Here are some four-star examples for which you must supply your own translations:

Ho-made pie

Utmost of chicken
  as Hungarian

Birds inwards parts

Pastry not special

Bowel of origan

Lumps with blight

Chicken smashed pot

Boiled steam

Glassy sheep bones

Thick intestine

Shrimbs lumps

Macaronis with ma

and all washed down with

Big rottle beer   and   Metallic water

CHICKEN SMASHED POT

mirabile dictu [Lat] (mih-RARB-ih-lay DIK-too)
Wonderful to relate.

mise-en-scène [Fr] The stage setting for a play.

Miserere [Lat] (mih-zer-AIR-ay) Have mercy. *Miserere mei,*
Deus – Have mercy on me, Lord: the 51st Psalm.

missa solemnis [Lat] (mis-suh soh-LEM-nis) Roman
Catholic High Mass.

Mist [Ger] Colloquially, 'manure' rather than 'shit'. Its
English equivalent would be 'rubbish'.

mistral [Fr] The notorious wind that blows from the Massif
Central across the south of France.

mit Gewalt [Ger] By force; by compulsion.

mit gleicher Münze zahlen [Ger] To repay tit for tat.

Mitteleuropa [Ger] Central Europe.

modus operandi [Lat] The way it works; method of operation.

modus vivendi [Lat] Agreement to differ; a compromise arrangement between two parties in dispute.

mœurs [Fr] Manners; customs.

moi non plus [Fr] Me neither.

moment de vérité [Fr] Moment of truth.

momzer [Yidd] Literally, bastard. A contemptible person.

mon ami [Fr] My friend. Feminine form is *mon amie*.

mon cher [Fr] My dear. Feminine form is *ma chère*.

mon chéri [Fr] My darling. Feminine form is *ma chérie*.

mon Dieu! [Fr] (mor(n) dyur) My God!

mont-de-piété [Fr] Licensed pawnshop, now known as *Crédit Municipal*. The equivalent in Spain is *monte de piedad,* and in Italy, *monte di pietà*.

Mord mit Messer und Gabel [Ger] Colloquial: death from over-eating.

Morgenstunde hat Gold im Munde [Ger] Literally, The morning has gold in its mouth. As the English version has it: 'Early to bed, early to rise, makes a man healthy, wealthy and wise.

morgue anglaise [Fr] English condescension.

morituri te salutant [Lat] We who are about to die salute you. This was the gladiatorial salute to the Roman emperors.

morta la bestia, morto il veneno [It] When the beast is dead he cannot bite.

mot juste See *le mot juste*.

motu proprio [Lat] Of one's free will.

moules [Fr] Mussels. *Moules marinières* – mussels served with a wine sauce.

mudéjar [Sp] Moorish-influenced architectural style in Spain.

muezzin [Arab] In Muslim countries, the crier who calls the faithful to prayer.

mucho en el suelo, poco en el cielo [Sp] Rich on earth, poor in the hereafter.

muito falar, pouco saber [Port] Many words, little knowledge.

mullah [Turk] A Muslim teacher, scholar or religious leader.

multa cadunt inter calicem supremaque labra [Lat] There's many a slip 'twixt cup and lip.

multi sunt vocati, pauci sunt electi [Lat] Many are called, few are chosen.

multis terribilis, caveto multos [Lat] If many fear you, beware of many.

multum in parvo [Lat] Much in a small space.

Mumienschänder [Ger] 'Mummy decorator'. A 'toy boy'; a young gigolo.

muor giovane colui ch'al cielo è caro [It] Whom the gods love dies young.

Murkin

There are an estimated 250 million users of Murkin, or American English. Although most users of British English have little trouble understanding basic Murkin, deep Murkin is something else; ***Kohl arnjews? Skedada'eer!*** (Cold orange juice? Let's get out of here!). A Murkin dictionary is no doubt in preparation, but meanwhile here's some help:

Texan Murkin	***bar*** – borrow; ***dense*** – dentist; ***mere*** – mirror
Brooklyn Murkin	***toidy-toid an' toid*** – Thirty-third and Third
Maryland Murkin	***Bollamuh*** – Baltimore; ***hoskul*** – high school; ***clays*** – clothes; ***par-me*** – pardon me

mutatis mutandis [Lat] The necessary or appropriate changes having been made.

mutilé de guerre [Fr] A disabled ex-serviceman.

Mütterchen [Ger] Grandma; old woman.

muu-muu [Haw] Light, loose, and often colourful dress.

muzhik; moujik; mujik [Rus] Russian peasant.

N

nach und nach [Ger] Little by little.

Nacktkultur (*also Freikörperkultur*) [Ger] Naturism; the cult of nudism.

Nagy-Britannia [Hung] Great Britain.

naïf [Fr] Artless; ingenuous.

naschen [Ger] To eat sweets when one shouldn't. The Yiddish term **nosh** (food) derives from this.

nasi goreng [Indonesian] Spiced rice dish topped with egg.

natura abhorret a vacuo [Lat] Nature abhors a vacuum.

natura il fece, e poi roppe la stampa [It] Nature made him, then broke the mould.

n'avoir pas le sou [Fr] To be without a sou; broke.

nazionale [It] *La Nazionale* – Italy's national football team. *Un nazionale* – an international player. For more on *il calcio* – Italy's national game – see *scudetto*.

nebech; nebbish [Yidd] A weak, ineffectual individual.

nec habeo, nec careo, nec curo [Lat] I have not, I want not, I care not.

ne choisitpas qui emprunte [Fr] He who borrows has no choice.

née [Fr] Literally, born. 'Her maiden name being'. Follows a woman's married name and indicates her original surname: Lucinda Black, *née* White.

nemine contradicente; nem. con. [Lat] With nobody dissenting; unanimously.

nemine dissentiente [Lat] Nobody dissents, nobody opposes.

nemo dat quod non habet [Lat] No-one can give what he does not possess.

nemo me impune lacessit [Lat] No-one injures me with impunity (motto of Scotland).

nemo mortalium omnibus horis sapit [Lat] No-one is wise at all times.

ne plus ultra [Lat] Literally, no more beyond. The pinnacle; the ultimate in perfection.

nessun dorma [It] None shall sleep. Title and opening line of the famous aria from Puccini's *Turandot* (and of B&B on Skye).

n'est-ce pas? [Fr] Isn't it?; isn't that so?

Neujahr [Ger] New Year.

Nicht alles, was glänzt ist Gold [Ger] All is not gold that glitters.

nihil ad rem [Lat] Irrelevant; not to the point.

Nihon [Jap] Japan. *Nihon-jin* – Japanese person. *Nihongo* – Japanese language. Another more widely known transliteration is *Nippon*.

nil carborundum illigitimi: [Liar's Latin] Don't let the bastards grind you down.

nil desperandum [Lat] Never despair.

nil mortalibus arduum est [Lat] Nothing is beyond the accomplishment of mortals.

nisi [Lat] (ny-sye) A decree that takes effect from a certain date unless cause is shown why it should not.

noblesse oblige [Fr] (noh-bless oh-BLEEZH) Originally the obligation of the nobility and aristocracy to act honourably; rank imposes obligations.

nochniye babochki [Rus] Literally, 'night butterflies'. Prostitutes on the streets of Moscow.

Noh; No [Jap] Elaborate stylized traditional Japanese
   drama.

noisette [Fr] (nwah-zet) Small, round boneless cut of
   lamb; hazelnut.

nolens volens [Lat] Whether willing or unwilling; having
   no alternative; willy-nilly.

noli irritare leones [Lat] Don't annoy the lions.

NO IRRITARE LEONES

noli me tangere [Lat] Do not touch me; a painting of
   Jesus appearing to Mary Magdalene after his
   resurrection.

nolle prosequi [Lat] Official abandonment of a legal action
   or a prosecution.

nom de guerre [Fr] (nom-duh-gair) An assumed name or
   pseudonym. The French equivalent of the anglicized
   nom de plume.

non compos mentis [Lat] Of unsound mind.

non generant aquilae columbas [Lat] Eagles do not bear doves.

non mi ricordo [It] I don't remember.

non possumus [Lat] (non pos-SOOM-us) Literally, we cannot. In law, inability to act in a matter.

non ragioniamo di loro, ma guarda e passa [It] From Dante: 'Speak not of them, but look and pass them by'.

non sapere l'abbicci [It] Literally, not to know the alphabet. To be abysmally ignorant.

non sequitur [Lat] Literally, it does not follow. A statement that does not follow logically from a preceding statement.

non so [It] I don't know – a phrase that infiltrates all everyday Italian speech as a 'sentence filler', equivalent to the English 'um y'know'.

Norwegian

Norway fascinates linguists because it has two written languages. After the dissolution of its union with Denmark in 1814 the country found itself saddled with Danish, which didn't fit at all with national aspirations. Throughout the nineteenth century Norway had to reinvent its own language, starting out with a mixture of Danish and native spoken Norwegian (**Riksmål**) and finishing up, at the end of the century, with **Bokmål,** or book language, and **Nynorsk,** or New Norwegian. Both are now taught in a bilingual Norway where the inhabitants customarily blend the two according to their geographic background and social status. Learning two languages may have honed their linguistic skills; a large number of Norwegians speak excellent English.

nos da [Welsh] Goodnight.

nostalgie de la boue [Fr] (literally 'nostaligia for the

mud') The perverse yearning of civilised people for
sordid and degrading experiences.

nota bene; NB [Lat] Note well; take notice.

Not bricht Eisen [Ger] Necessity breaks iron; equivalent to
'necessity is the mother of invention'.

nous [Gk] Reason. Colloquially, in English, it means
common sense or intelligence.

nous verrons ce que nous verrons [Fr] We shall see
what we shall see.

nouveau riche [Fr] (noo-voh reesh) Someone who has
recently become wealthy but is regarded as socially
inferior.

novus homo [Lat] A new man; an *arriviste*; an upstart.

nuda veritas [Lat] Naked truth.

nudis verbis [Lat] In plain words.

nudnik [Yidd] A bore.

nul bien sans peine [Fr] No pain, no gain.

nulla mensa sine impensa [Lat] There's no free lunch.

nulla nulla [Abor] Club used as a weapon by Australian
aborigines.

nulla nuova, buona nuova [It] No news is good news.

nulli desperandum, quamdiu spirat [Lat] While there's
life, there's hope.

nulli secundus [Lat] Second to none.

nullo modo [Lat] No way!

nunc aut nunquam [Lat] Now or never.

nunc dimittis [Lat] From the first line of the Latin version
of Simeon's Canticle: 'Lord, now lettest thou thy
servant depart in peace'.

nunc est bibendum [Lat] Now is the time for drinking.

nunquam dormio [Lat] I never sleep; I am always on my
guard. Motto of *The Observer* newspaper.

nyet [Rus] No.

o

obi [Jap] The wide sash with a bow at the back, worn as part of their national costume by Japanese women.

obiter dictum [Lat] (OB-ih-tur DIK-tum) An incidental comment or observation. In law, a relevant observation on a point of law by a judge, but not binding.

objet d'art [Fr] (ob-zhay dar) A work of art.

objets d'occasion [Fr] Second-hand goods.

obscurum per obscurius [Lat] Trying to explain some obscure point by referring to something even more obscure.

ocha [Jap] Japanese tea. *Kocha* – Indian tea

oderint dum metuant [Lat] Let them hate, so long as they fear.

odi et amo [Lat] I hate and love; the 'love-hate' syndrome.

o Dio! [It] Common Italian expression meaning, roughly, Good Lord! Good heavens! Blimey!

odium scholasticum [Lat] The bitter disagreements among scholars. *Odium theologicum* – acrimonious debate between theologians. Similar for *odium medicum* (doctors) and *odium aestheticum* (aesthetics).

oeil-de-boeuf [Fr] (UH-ee duh-buhf) Small round window in seventeenth- and eighteenth-century (French) buildings.

oeuf [Fr] (uhf) Egg. **oeufs brouillés** – scrambled eggs;

oeuf dur – hard-boiled egg; *oeuf poché* – poached egg; *oeuf sur le plat* – fried egg; *une omelette* – omelette.

oeuvre [Fr] (urv-ruh) The output of work, usually by a writer or artist.

ogni medaglia ha il suo rovescio [It] There are two sides to every medal (or coin).

ohne Wissen, ohne Sünde [Ger] Without knowledge, without sin.

¡olé!

This expression is now semi-anglicised and most of us believe it means – approximately – 'Bravo!' 'Fantastic!' or some other shout of encouragement during a performance.

But ¡olé! is rather more than that; it is, especially at a flamenco performance, a deeply-felt, emotional expression of appreciation, generally shouted towards the end of a movement and as much part of the show as the music and dancing. It really means 'By God!' and is perhaps closer to the biblical 'hallelujah!' than to the meaning we have given it.

oleum addere camino [Lat] Adding fuel to the fire.

olio [Sp] Meat and vegetable stew. In Italian, **olio** – oil; **olio d'oliva** – olive oil.

omadhaun [Ir] A fool; an idiot.

omertà [It] Code of silence among members of a criminal fraternity, especially the Mafia.

omnem movere lapidem [Lat] Leave no stone unturned.

omnia ad Dei gloriam [Lat] All things to the glory of God.

omnia mors aequat [Lat] Death levels all.

omnia vincit amor [Lat] (om-nih-uh vin-kit ah-mor) Love conquers everything. **Omnia vincit labor** – labour conquers everything.

on dit [Fr] (o(n) dee) Literally, it is said. Gossip; rumour.

onus probandi [Lat] The burden of proof; it is up to the accuser to prove the allegation.

omofilofilos [Gk] Homosexual. **Haroomenos** – gay, but in its traditional meaning of 'happy' or 'lighthearted'.

ouzeri [Gk] Greek bar that serves ouzo and beer with *mezés,* or snacks.

opéra bouffe [Fr] (op-ay-ruh boof) Comic opera.

opera buffa [It] (op-er-ruh boof-uh) Comic opera.

opere citato [Lat] In the work quoted already; often seen in footnotes as the abbreviation *op cit*.

opéra comique [Fr] (op-ay-ruh com-eek) Light opera, often comic, with spoken dialogue.

opus Dei [Lat] (oh-pus day-ih) The work of God.

ora et labora [Lat] Pray and work.

ora pro nobis [Lat] Pray for us.

orbis terrarum [Lat] The earth.

ordre du jour [Fr] Order of the day; the agenda.

oshibori [Jap] The moist cloth for wiping hands before a meal.

osteria [It] An inn.

O tempora! O mores! [Lat] Oh, what times! Oh, what manners! A traditional lament at falling standards of behaviour.

Oubykh and other dying languages

Oubykh, an unusual language with just three vowels but eighty consonants, was never an important language. It was, when first recorded, spoken by only 50,000 or so Caucasian people inhabiting the regions of South West Russia between the Caspian and Black seas. Now there are none: the last Oubykh native speaker is believed to have died around 1989.

Dozens of languages are under threat. One is Ulithi, spoken on a remote Micronesian island by only seventy people. But even Ulithi has done better than Manx, now extinct, and Cornish, which lost its last native speaker a couple of centuries ago. This did not, however, discourage schoolmaster Melville Bennetto from publishing the first novel in Cornish in 1984. 'I'm not expecting to make a fortune,' he said; 'there are only a couple of hundred people in the world who can understand it'.

Are Welsh and Gaelic on the endangered list? With handsome government subsidies, Welsh is thriving. So is the community of some 80,000 Scots Gaelic speakers, as shown by the opening in Glasgow in 1999 of the first wholly Gaelic-medium school in Scotland. But in Ireland, where about 1% of the population regularly use Gaelic, the picture is far from rosy. Despite government subsidies, even its most enthusiastic champions fear that its existence as a living language may not long persist into the 21st century.

---

oui [Fr] (wee) Yes. The correct or authentically French pronunciation of **oui** is one of the most difficult of all to master.

outrance [Fr] Extreme; the last extremity; excess.
Outrancier – extremist.

outré [Fr] (oo-tray) Exaggerated; excessive; eccentric; extravagant.

ouvrage de longue haleine [Fr] Literally, a work of long breath. A long, sustained achievement.

P

pace [Lat] (pah-chay *also* pah-say or pay-see) Preceding a person's name, it expresses polite disagreement about some point, but with apologies.

paella [Sp] (English version; in Spanish, pa-EY-a) A mixed dish of chicken, shellfish and perhaps other meats with rice.

pain [Fr] Bread, in various shapes and sizes: *baquette, ficelle, bâtard, saucisson,* etc. **Le pain grillé** – toast.

palazzo [It] (pa-LAT-zoh) Originally 'palace' but now any large mansion or building. **Palazzo municipale** – town hall.

palmam qui meruit ferat [Lat] Let him bear the palm who has deserved it.

panem et circenses [Lat] Bread and circuses (for the masses).

pannekoekhuisje [Dut] Pancake house, serving up to fifty different kinds of these Dutch specialities.

paparazzo [It] The ugly side of photography; 'sneak' news photographer. Plural: *paparazzi.*

papier [Fr] (pap-yay) Paper. **Papier hygiénique** – toilet paper; **papier de soie** – tissue paper; **papier machine (à écrire)** – typing paper.

papillon [Fr] Literally, butterfly. Colloquially, a parking ticket.

papillote [Fr] Buttered paper used to wrap meat or fish, which is then baked.

par avion [Fr] By airmail.

para todo hay remedio sino para la muerte [Sp] There is a remedy for everything but death.

parbleu [Fr] My God! Euphemism for *par Dieu*.

par excellence [Fr] Pre-eminently; above all.

par exemple [Fr] For instance.

pari mutuel [Fr] A type of betting or lottery in which the winners share the available stake.

pari passu [Lat] With equal speed; simultaneously.

paroles en l'air [Fr] Idle words; pointless discussion.

partager le gâteau [Fr] To share the cake; split the takings.

partie carrée [Fr] (par-tee kar-ray) A group of four people, customarily two couples.

parti pris [Fr] (par-tee PREE) A preconceived opinion; prejudiced.

parvenu [Fr] Someone who, becoming wealthy and having risen socially, is considered to be an unsuitable member of his or her new class. Feminine: *parvenue*.

pas de chat [Fr] A ballet dancer's catlike leap.

pas de deux [Fr] A ballet dance for two dancers.

Pas de deux (father of twins) and more Fractured French

Like Liar's Latin, inventing Fractured French – coming up with new definitions for well-known phrases and sayings – is a pastime that's been around for generations, so don't be surprised if some of the examples below are a bit *passé*.

hors de combat – prostitute wrestlers
coup de grâce – lawnmower
tant mieux – spinster cat

entrechat – cat flap

après moi le déluge – June is the rainiest month

carte de visite – tourist bus

crêpe de chine – doggie droppings

tête-à-tête – a tight bra

tour de force – join the army, see the world

nostalgie de la boue – bring back those old horror films

levée en masse – let them eat unleavened bread

rien n'arrive pour rien – when it rains it pours

vol-au-vent – wind in the stomach

eau de toilette – water from the loo

moi aussi – I am Australian

---

pas devant les enfants [Fr] (pah duh-vah(n) layz ah(n)-fah(n)) Not in front of the children.

pas glissé [Fr] Dance term; Gliding, sliding step.

passer une nuit blanche [Fr] Literally, to pass a white night. To have a sleepless night.

passim [Lat] Here and there; in many places. Usually a footnote to show that a reference occurs throughout a book.

pasto [It] Meal. **Antipasto** – hors d'œuvre.

pastrami [Yidd] Smoked, seasoned beef.

patchouli [Tamil] Fragrant oil and perfume from the leaves of the Pogostemon, an Asian tree.

paterfamilias [Lat] The Father; head of the household.

pâtisserie [Fr] French cake shop.

pavé [Fr] Literally, a paving stone. Colloquially, a large thick steak.

pax Britannica [Lat] Peace imposed by the British during the empire period.

pax vobiscum [Lat] Peace be with you.

paysage [Fr] (pay-zahzh) Landscape; landscape painting.

peccavi [Lat] (peh-KAH-vee) I have sinned. It is used lightheartedly as an apology. And as a pun; when

British Army general Sir Charles Napier captured the Indian province of Sind he sent HQ a telegram which simply said *Peccavi*.

pedir peras al olmo [Sp] Don't try to find pears on an elm; don't expect the impossible.

peignoir [Fr] (pen-wahr) A woman's loose dressing-gown.

peintre de dimanche [Fr] A 'Sunday painter'; an amateur artist.

pelota [Sp] Game played by two players with small baskets strapped to their wrists to hurl a ball at a marked wall. See **jai alai,** a similar game.

pendejo [Sp] Literally, a pubic hair, but used colloquially to mean a fool; an idiot.

pensa molto, parla poco, e scrivi meno [It] Think much, talk little, and write less.

pensée [Fr] (pah(n)-say) A thought expressed in elegant writing.

pentimento [It] Revealing an addition or alteration made by an artist to a painting; revealing something previously hidden.

per capita [Lat] Literally, by heads. For or by each person.

per diem [Lat] Each day.

père [Fr] Father.

perestroika [Rus] (peh-rih-STROY-kuh) The reform and restructuring of the political and economic system of the former Soviet Union in the 1980s.

perfide Albion [Fr] Treacherous England. A traditional view held by the French.

per incuriam [Lat] By negligence; by oversight.

per procurationem; per pro; pp [Lat] By proxy; by delegation to. The abbreviation *pp* is used by someone signing a letter or document on behalf of another.

per se [Lat] (pur say) In itself; by itself; essentially.

persona non grata [Lat] A person who is unacceptable or unwelcome.

pesca [It] Peach; but also fishing. **Pesce** – fish.

pesto [It] A paste or sauce based on basil, often served with pasta.

pétanque [Fr] Another name for the game of **boules**.

pet-de-nonne [Fr] Literally, nun's fart. A light cake made with choux pastry.

péter [Fr] To fart. **Péter le feu** – to fart fire; to be full of energy.

PÉTER LE FEU

pétillant [Fr] Describes wine that is slightly effervescent.

petit ami [Fr] Boyfriend. **Petite amie** – girlfriend.

petite bourgeoisie [Fr] (puh-teet boor-zhwah-zee) The lower middle classes. **Petit bourgeois** – a member of this class, usually used in a derogatory sense.

petit maître [Fr] A dandy or toff.

petits fours [Fr] (peh-tih FOOR) Fancily iced small cakes.

petits pois [Fr] (peh-tih PWAH) Small, fresh green peas.

phrase toute faite [Fr] A cliché; a common phrase.

piac [Hung] (py-ut) Hungarian open market. The biggest and best-known is the *Bosnyák téri piac* in Budapest.

pibroch [Gael] A theme with variations for the Scottish bagpipe.

picante [Sp] Hot; highly peppered and spiced. **Picantería** – restaurant specializing in hot food.

piccola morte [It] Literally, little death. An orgasm; a state of drug-induced oblivion.

Pidgin

Pidgin is a language formed from the vocabularies and grammars of other languages in order to facilitate communication between speakers of many different languages.

One of the most interesting pidgins today is Melanesian pidgin, the lingua franca of Papua New Guinea (which has some 600 mother tongues), Solomon Islands, Vanuatu and other islands of Melanesia. It is also the official language of the Papua New Guinea parliament and has a full grammatical structure. The number of people who use only pidgin, and who regard it as their mother tongue, is growing.

To speakers of English, the vocabulary of pidgin can seem strangely, even comically, familiar. The structure of the language leads to some vivid, seemingly incongruous juxtapositions. You may experience the shock of recognition in the following phrases:

ashes	*shit bilong faia*
moustache	*gras bilong maus* (mouth)
broken, ruined	*bagarup* (buggered-up)
house foundations	*ars bilong haus* (arse – bottom)
sexual intercourse	*push pushim*
of no consequence	*samting nating* (something nothing)
hurricane lamp	*lam wokabout*

Just as graphic but more economical are these instructions for using western toilets (*Hao Yu Usim Kloset*):

1. *Putim daon sit bilong kloset*

2. *Sidaon long maos bilong kloset*

3. *Taem yu finis flusim kloset*

4. *Wasem han bilong yu*

---

pièce de résistance [Fr] The principal or special creation of an artist, performer or chef.

pied-à-terre [Fr] (pyay-dah-TAIR) Not a main residence, but usually a convenient town or city flat.

Pietà [It] The image of the Virgin Mary holding the dead body of Christ.

pijiu [Ch] Beer.

pila in area tua est [Lat] The ball is in your court.

piña colada [Sp] A long drink made with rum, pineapple juice and coconut.

pinxit [Lat] He/she painted it.

pipi de chat [Fr] (pee-pee duh shah) Cat's pee. Used by wine experts to describe the pungent aroma of wine made from the Sauvignon blanc grape. Also used colloquially to mean an unpleasantly rancid drink.

pique [Fr] (peek) A display of resentment or irritation.

piqué [Fr] (pee-kay) Ribbed fabric of cotton and silk.

piropos [Sp] The 'compliments' shouted to women by Hispanic males: the articulated and often explicit equivalent to the admiring whistle which a woman is supposed to ignore.

pis aller [Fr] (pee zah-lay) A last resort, in the absence of anything better.

piscem natare docere [Lat] Teaching a fish how to swim.

piscine [Fr] Swimming pool.

pissoir [Fr] (pee-swahr) A public urinal.

piste [Fr] A ski-run, slope or course.

pisto [Sp] Traditional Spanish dish of vegetables fried in olive oil. Do not confuse with **pito,** which is slang for penis.

place au soleil, une [Fr] A place in the sun.

plage [Fr] (plazh) A bathing beach.

plat du jour [Fr] (plah doo ZHOOR) A restaurant's dish of the day.

plein air [Fr] In the open air; a school of landscape painting.

plus ça change, plus c'est la même chose [Fr] (ploo sah shah(n)zh, ploo say lah mehm shohz) The more things change, the more they stay the same. Often shortened to **plus ça change**.

Poetic licence

In a magazine article on Australia, a well-known English poet commented on the cry of the Western Australian Twenty-eight parrot, so named, he said, because its call sounded like 'twenty-eight, twenty-eight'.

Either the poetic ear was on holiday or something was lost in translation. The bird was, in fact, first described by a

French ornithologist who reported, correctly, that its call sounded like **vingt-huit, vingt-huit** (vah(n)t-weet, vah(n)t-weet), which, of course, means twenty-eight, twenty-eight in French!

---

poi [Haw] A dish made from fermented taro root.

pointillisme [Fr] Style of painting, made famous by Seurat, which uses multi-coloured dots to achieve an impressionistic effect.

polenta [It] Thick maize porridge.

polizia [It] Italian police. **Metropolitani** – Municipal police; **Corpo della Pubblica Sicurezza** – Public police; **Pubblica Siccurezza** and **Carabinieri** – Military police; **Guardia di Finanza** – Customs police; **Polizia Giudiziaria** – Criminal Investigation Department; **polizia stradale** – traffic police; **vigili notturni** – private security guards.

pommes frites [Fr] (pom freet) French fries; chips.

portière [Fr] The anti-draught curtain behind a door.

posada [Sp] Spanish inn.

poste restante [Fr] (post RES-tah(n)t) Section of a post office that keeps mail for collection, e.g. by people on holiday.

post meridiem; p.m. [Lat] After noon; afternoon.

post nubila, Phoebus [Lat] After clouds, the sun.

post obitum [Lat] After death.

postpartum [Lat] After childbirth.

post scriptum; PS [Lat] An addition or note added below the signature.

potage [Fr] Soup.

pot-au-feu [Fr] Boiled beef in broth.

pot-pourri [Fr] (poh-poo-ree) A miscellany; a medley; a mixed collection; specifically a mixture of dried, fragrant rose and other flower petals.

pourboire [Fr] (poor-bwahr) A tip; gratuity.

pour encourager les autres [Fr] To encourage the rest. People often use this ironically, as did its originator, Voltaire, in commenting on the execution by the Royal Navy of its Admiral Byng for negligence in 1757.

pour épater les bourgeois [Fr] To shock the middle classes.

pourquoi? [Fr] Why?

pour rire [Fr] In fun; not to be taken seriously.

pousse-café [Fr] Literally, push-coffee. A liqueur drunk after dinner, with or just after coffee.

précieuse [Fr] (pray-syurz) Precious; affected.

préciosité [Fr] (pray-sios-ih-tay) Extreme affectation.

prego [It] (pray-goh) The equivalent of 'don't mention it', said to someone who thanks you.

prêt-à-porter [Fr] Ready to wear.

prima donna [It] Literally, first lady. A female opera star; also someone who is temperamental and difficult to deal with.

prima facie [Lat] (pree-mah fay-sih) At first sight; in law, using available but not necessarily complete or tested evidence to arrive at a conclusion.

primus inter pares [Lat] First among equals; having precedence but only equal authority.

pris sur le fait [Fr] Caught in the act.

prix d'ami [Fr] A 'special price' for a friend.

prix fixe [Fr] An inclusive fixed price, usually for a meal.

pro bono (publico), [Lat] For the public good, not for a fee.

profanum vulgus [Lat] The herd; the common multitude.

pro forma [Lat] According to procedure; as a matter of form. A *pro forma* invoice is one issued before purchase and delivery of the goods.

pro rata [Lat] In proportion; proportionally.

pro rege et patria [Lat] For king and country.

prosit! [Lat] Good health! German and other languages

have it as **prost!**; the Dutch is **proost!**

pro tempore; pro tem [Lat] For the time being; temporarily.

prudens futuri [Lat] Thinking of the future.

psaria [Gk] Fish. **Psarotaverna** – fish restaurant.

psistaria [Gk] Restaurant specializing in charcoal grills.

puîné [Fr] Younger. **Puisné** – Old French, meaning 'born later' from which is derived the class of judges known as puisne judges, i.e. of lower rank.

puissance [Fr] (pwee-sah(n)s) Show-jumping competition to test a horse's ability over a series of close high jumps.

pukka [Hindi] Properly done; genuine.

puta [Sp] Whore, and a common vulgarism. *Hijo de puta* is one of the top ten Hispanic insults (**hijo** – son).

putsch [Ger] (pootch) A violent overthrow of authority.

Q

qarwah [Arab] Coffee.

Quai d'Orsay [Fr] (kay-DOR-say) The French Foreign
Ministry.

qualche volta è virtù facere il vero [It] Sometimes it is a
virtue to conceal the truth.

qualis vita, finis ita [Lat] As in life, so is the end.

Quartier Latin [Fr] The Paris bohemian south bank area.

quattrocento [It] The period from 1400 to 1500 (see
cinquecento); art of that period.

Quebec's tongue troopers

The French-speaking holdout in Canada is Quebec where,
since 1976, Bill 101, the province's French-language charter,
and Bill 178, the sign law, have banned all languages other
than French from public life in Quebec. The Draconian
language laws are administered by the *Commission de
Surveillance de la Langue Française,* unpopularly known as
the 'vocabulary constabulary' or the 'tongue troopers'.
Quebec government officials are empowered to inspect
business premises and documents without search warrants
and impose fines for use of English-only signs.

The laws have been only partly successful and are
generally scorned, especially by the 800,000 Québecois who
speak English. One town – named Buckingham, after its

English counterpart – was fined for defying an order to remove the words 'Town Hall' from its town hall. A consignment of kosher food fell foul of the authorities because its labelling was not in French. Quebec's efforts to control the language of the people seem, like similar efforts in the past, to be doomed: English-speaking people are leaving, the birth rate of the French-speaking population is falling, and fewer immigrants are arriving.

---

que besa sus pies [Sp] Literally, who kisses your feet. Shortened to **QBSP** it is a writer's fond sign-off in a letter to a woman.

quenelle [Fr] Seasoned, fried meat or fish ball.

¿qué pasó? [Sp] Colloquial greeting equivalent to 'how's it going?' or 'what's happening?'

quequette; quiquette [Fr] Vulgar slang for penis.

que sais-je? [Fr] What do I know?

que será será [Sp] (kay suh-RAR suh-RAR) What will be will be.

que ta casquette ne sache ta guise [Fr] Don't let even your cap know what thoughts it covers.

quid pro quo [Lat] Something for something; an equitable exchange.

quieta non movere [Lat] Let sleeping dogs lie.

qui m'aime aime mon chien [Fr] Who loves me loves my dog; Love me, love my dog.

quincaillerie [Fr] An ironmonger's shop, or the hardware and utensils sold there.

quinta [Sp] In Spain, originally a country house, but now usually a suburban villa.

quis custodiet ipsos custodes? [Lat] Who will guard the guards?

qui s'excuse s'accuse [Fr] He who makes excuses for himself accuses himself.

Quittung [Ger] Receipt.

qui vive [Fr] (kee-veev) The alert.

quod erat demonstrandum; QED [Lat] That which was
to be demonstrated or proved.

quod vide; q.v. [Lat] Which see. The abbreviation *q.v.* is
used to advise readers to consult other references on the
subject in the same work.

quo vadis? [Lat] Whither goest thou?

R

Rache trägt keine Frucht [Ger] Revenge brings no fruit.

radschlagen [Ger] To perform a gymnastic cartwheel. **Die Düsseldorfer Radschläger** – the cartwheel performances on the Königstraße, well known to tourists.

raffreddore [It] The common cold in Italy; colloquially known as catching a _freddo_.

ragoût [Fr] (rah-goo) Highly seasoned stew.

raison d'état [Fr] Reason(s) of state; for the state's security.

raison d'être [Fr] (ray-zoh(n) det-ruh) Reason for existing.

râle de la mort [Fr] Death rattle, the rough breathing of a dying person.

Ramadan [Arab] The religious thirty-day sunrise-to-sunset fast in the ninth month of the Muslim year.

rapporteur [Fr] Someone directed to investigate and to submit a report on the findings.

rapprochement [Fr] (rah-PROSH-mah(n)) A coming together; establishing or re-establishing friendly relations.

rara avis [Lat] (rah-ruh AY-vis) Literally, rare bird. Something or someone most unusual and rarely encountered.

RARA AVIS

Rasthaus [Ger] Small motel by main roads and the
Autobahnen in which travellers can rest for a few
hours.

ratatouille [Fr] (raht-ah-TWEE) Fried and stewed
vegetable casserole.

Rathaus [Ger] (RAH-tows) German town hall.

Ratskeller [Ger] Upmarket restaurant, as distinct from the
Gastkeller where drinkers are likely to outnumber
diners.

rav [Heb] Rabbi.

Realpolitik [Ger] Politics based on practicalities and opportunism rather than ideals and morals.

rebozo [Sp] Shawl worn by Hispanic women over their heads and shoulders.

réchauffé [Fr] (ray-shoh-fay) Warmed up leftovers; anything rehashed from old, stale materials.

recherché [Fr] (ruh-SHAIR-shay) Refined and rare; obscure.

réclame [Fr] (ray-KLAHM) Self-advertisement; publicity-seeking; a talent for notoriety.

reculer pour mieux sauter [Fr] A strategic retreat in order to make a more effective advance.

rédacteur [Fr] Publishing editor. **Rédaction** – editing.

Reden ist Silber, Schweigen ist Gold [Ger] Speech is silver, silence is gold.

reductio ad absurdum [Lat] To prove the falsity of a proposition by demonstrating that its logical conclusion is absurd.

règlement [Fr] The rule or regulation. **Il faut agir selon les règlements** – you must conform to the rules.

Reich [Ger] (rykh) German empire or state. Specifically, the **First Reich** (962-1806 or Bismarck's empire of 1871-1919); **Second Reich** (Weimar Republic, 1919-1933); **Third Reich** (Nazi Germany, 1933-1945).

relais routier [Fr] (reh-lay root-yay) Roadside restaurant and rest-place used by travellers and lorry drivers.

relata refero [Lat] I tell it as it was told to me.

religieuse [Fr] Nun. **Religieux** – monk or brother.

reliquiae [Lat] Remains, especially fossils of animals or plants.

remonte-pente [Fr] Ski-lift.

rémoulade [Fr] Herb mayonnaise sauce for salads.

renaissance [Fr] Rebirth; revival. **Renaissance** – classical revival in the fifteenth-sixteenth centuries.

renkött [Swed] Reindeer.

renommé [Fr] Celebrated; famous.

rentier [Fr] (rah(n)t-yay) Someone who lives off investments or has independent means.

repas maigre [Fr] Vegetarian (meatless) meal.

repêchage [Fr] (reh-peh-sharzh) A heat in a contest in which runners-up in previous heats compete for a place in the final.

répondez, s'il vous plaît; RSVP [Fr] (ray-poh(n)-day seel voo play) Reply if you please.

requiescat in pace; RIP [Lat] (rek-wih-ES-kat in pah-chay) May he/she rest in peace.

retroussé [Fr] (ruh-TROO-say) Turned up nose.

revanche [Fr] (ruh-VANSH) Literally, revenge.
Revanchisme – policy of retaliation to regain something lost.

réveillon [Fr] French Christmas and New Year's celebrations usually involving meals and drinks after midnight.

revenons à nos moutons [Fr] Literally, let's return to our sheep. Let's return to the subject; let's get back to the point.

rex non potest peccare [Lat] The king can do no wrong.

Rhyming slang

The Times authority on English, Philip Howard, tells of an exchange he had with a newsvendor on the London Underground. 'How are you?' he asked. He was told: 'Cold – this perishin' wind's blowin' straight up me plaster!'

Plaster? Eventually Howard traced it back: **plaster – Plaster of Paris – arris – Aristotle – bottle – bottle and glass – arse.**

That's Cockney rhyming slang *in extremis*. Most of it is simply one rhyme removed, as with these well-known examples: **titfer – tit for tat – hat; boracic – boracic lint**

– **skint** (or **broke**); **frog** – **frog and toad** – **road; syrup** –
syrup of fig – **wig**.

Rhyming slang sometimes takes on the qualities of a
foreign language, in that you can't understand it. Here are a
few examples that can have you guessing:

barnet – **Barnet Fair** – **hair**
harvey – **Harvey Nichols** – **pickles**
linen – **linen draper** – **paper** – **newspaper**
Kate and Sidney – **steak and kidney**
sweene – **Sweeney Todd** – **the Flying Squad**
oxo – **Oxo cube** – **tube(/Underground)**

The more streetwise readers will need no help with **fun
and frolics, khyber,** and **orchestras**.

---

ride bene chi ride l'ultimo [It] He laughs best who laughs
   last.
ridere in stomacho [Lat] To laugh up your sleeve.
rien ne va plus [Fr] No more bets. The roulette croupier's
   announcement before spinning the wheel.
rijstafel [Dut] (rays-tah-fel) Indonesian banquet based on
   rice with a variety of vegetables and meats.
rincer les yeux [Fr] 'Eyewash'; colloquial for an admiring
   gaze at an attractive object, usually a woman.
ripopée [Fr] Dregs; slops; what's left.
rira bien qui rira le dernier [Fr] He laughs best who
   laughs last.
rive gauche [Fr] (reev gohsh) The left bank of the Seine in
   Paris; the Latin Quarter.
rivière [Fr] Multi-stringed necklace of precious stones.
robe de chambre [Fr] (rohb duh shah(n)-bruh) Dressing-
   gown.
roman à clef [Fr] (roh-mah(n) ah clay) A novel which
   describes real events and has real people as characters.
romanesco; romano [It] The dialect of Rome.
roman-fleuve [Fr] Series of novels about one group or family.

romanista [It] A Rome Football Club supporter. The other Roman team is the Lazio FC or the *biancoazzurri*, whose supporters are called *laziale*.

rompiscatole [It] Literally, ball-breaker. Vulgar for a bore, pest or nuisance.

rondelet; rondelette [Fr] Plump; chubby; a well-rounded person.

rondine [It] A swallow. *Una rondine non fa primavera* – one swallow doesn't make a spring.

Rosh Hashanah [Heb] (rohsh hah-SHAH-nuh) Jewish New Year.

rôti [Fr] (roh-tee) In cooking, to roast; roasted food.

roublard [Fr] Cunning; a sharp character.

roué [Fr] (roo-ay) A lecherous, debauched male.

roux [Fr] (roo) Blend of butter or other fat and flour, used as the basis for sauces.

rusé [Fr] (roo-zay) Wily; tricky; cunning.

rus in urbe [Lat] (roos in UR-bay) Bringing the country to the city; the creation of rural atmosphere in a town.

Russian

Modern Russian is absorbing English words and terms at a breathtaking rate and the language is now so *heavily invaded* by English *jargon*, slang and *tekhnologiya* that the Western visitor can have the feeling of making passable progress without recourse to the native tongue. Which, perhaps, is just as well: with its upside-down-reversed-looking alphabet, complex grammar and palatal pronunciation, Russian can't be an easy language to master.

But with so many English-flavoured words in the modern vocabulary it's almost possible to read a Russian newspaper, where you'll come across *rok* (rock), *dzhaz* (jazz), *dzinzi* (jeans), *kaseta* (cassette), *shuz* (shoes), *vash* (watch) and even a *finalny match* of *basketbolny*. What

was once a *vychislitelnaya mashina* is now a *kompyuter.*
Efficiency is *effektivnost* and gangsters are *gangstery.* And
striptease is, surprise, surprise – *striptiz.*

---

ryokan [Jap] Traditional Japanese inns in which guests can
experience local food and customs.

S

sacré bleu! [Fr] Curse it! Confound it!

sain et sauf [Fr] Safe and sound.

salaam [Arab] (sah-LAHM) Peace. A Muslim salutation.

salaud [Fr] (sah-LOH) Bastard; swine; sod, etc. *Petit salaud* – little bastard.

salata horiatiki [Gr] Greek salad.

salière [Fr] Salt-cellar.

salle à manger [Fr] (sal-ah-mah(n) zhay) Dining-room.

salle d'attente [Fr] (sal dah-tah(n)t) Waiting-room.

salope [Fr] A bitch.

salsa [Sp] Spicy Latin American sauce. Also a kind of dance music.

saltimbanque [Fr] A quack; crook.

saltimbocca [It] Herbed dish of folded veal and prosciutto.

salvete [Lat] Welcome! Greetings!

salvo pudore [Lat] Without offence to modesty.

salwar kameez [Urdu] The outfit of tunic and loose trousers worn by many Indian and Pakistani women.

samadhi [Hindi] An ultimate trance-like state in yoga.

samizdat [Rus] Self-published; published clandestinely.

san [Jap] The word you add to all Japanese surnames (which in Japan are written first: with Harawa Keiko, Harawa is the surname; Keiko is the given name) which is the all-purpose equivalent of Mr, Mrs and Ms.

sanctum sanctorum [Lat] The holy of holies; a private sanctum.

sang-froid [Fr] (sah(n) frwah) Composure; calmness; self-possession.

sans [Fr] (Eng pronunciation: 'sanz' (not 'so (n)) Without.

sans blague [Fr] (sah(n) blahg) Without joking; seriously.

sans-culotte [Fr] (sah(n)-koo-LOT) Originally a poor revolutionary; any republican extremist.

sans doute [Fr] Without doubt.

sans façon [Fr] (sah(n) fah-soh(n)) Unceremoniously; brusquely.

sans gêne [Fr] (sah(n) zhehn) Disregard for politeness; when someone is offending without realizing it.

sans peur et sans reproche [Fr] Without fear and above reproach.

sans prétensions [Fr] Unpretentious; unaffected.

santé [Fr] (sah(n)-tay) Good health.

Sartor Resartus [Lat] The tailor mended (from Thomas Carlyle's book of 1834).

sashimi [Jap] Varieties of raw fish served as a meal.

SASHIMI

Sassenach [Scot] An English person or lowlander.
satis eloquentiae, sapientae parum [Lat] Abounding
  eloquence, scant wisdom.
saucisse; saucisson [Fr] The former is an uncooked
  sausage; the latter is a cooked sausage for eating cold.

A *saucière* of sauces

The great French cook Alexis Soyer once wrote that 'Sauces
are to cookery what grammar is to language'. This was
about the time that England was reviled as a 'nation with
one sauce' but since then things – and sauces – have moved
on a bit and the average British diner today is familiar with
at least a few of them. Are you?

Sauce à la menthe	mint
Sauce allemande	butter, flour, lemon juice, nutmeg
Sauce au beurre	butter
Sauce aux câpres	capers
Sauce aux cornichons	brown sauce with gherkins
Sauce béarnaise	egg yolks, butter, vinegar and tarragon
Sauce béchamel	white roux with seasoning – the foundation of many other sauces
Sauce bordelaise	with claret, shallots, seasoning
Sauce bretonne	simple egg and butter sauce
Sauce espagnole	thick basic brown sauce
Sauce financière	with madeira or sherry
Sauce génoise	fish stock, anchovy butter, claret
Sauce hollandaise	warmed egg yolks, butter, lemon
Sauce meunière	butter, parsley, lemon juice

Sauce mousseline	*sauce hollandaise* with whipped cream
Sauce régence	fish stock and Marsala wine
Sauce tartare	for fish and seafood
Sauce tournée	with onions and mushrooms
Sauce valois	egg yolks, vinegar, shallots
Sauce velouté	a variation of béchamel
Sauce zwetschen	prunes, port, lemon juice, cinnamon

säufer [Ger] Drunkard; alcoholic. *Er säuft wie ein Loch* – someone who 'drinks like a fish'.

Sauregurkenzeit [Ger] Literally, pickled gherkin time – a period when nothing is happening in business or politics. Known elsewhere as the 'silly season'.

sauve-qui-peut [Fr] Literally, save himself who can. A situation of panic and disorder in which it is every man for himself.

savoir-faire [Fr] (sav-wahr FAIR) Polish; tact; the ability to do the right thing when required.

savoir-vivre [Fr] (sav-wahr VEEV-ruh) Ease; composure; the quality of being at ease in society.

sayonara [Jap] Goodbye.

sbirro [It] Colloquial for Italian policeman.

scappatella [It] Flirtation; brief extra-marital relationship.

schadenfreude [Ger] (SHAH-den-froy-duh) A fashionable word of the 1990s meaning taking malicious pleasure from another's misfortune. Until relatively recently, as a non-anglicised word it would have carried a capital *S*.

schemozzle [Yidd] (shih-MOZZ-ul) A mix-up; mess; argument.

Schickse [Ger] Tart; trollop.

schifo [It] Disgust. *Mi far schifo* – it makes me sick! A widely used colloquial word for complaining.

Schlafen Sie wohl! [Ger] Sleep well!

Schlager [Ger] Pop song; a musical hit.

schlemiel [Yidd] (shluh-MEEL) A simple person, usually a man, who has the best intentions but no luck; unlucky but uncomplaining.

schlep; shlep [Yidd] To drag or carry with effort.

schlimmbesserung [Ger] An improvement that makes things worse.

schlock [Yidd] Cheap; inferior; rubbish; in bad taste.

Schloss [Ger] A German castle; a country estate.

shmaltz [Yidd] Sugary sentimentality.

shmuck [Yidd] Someone who always does the wrong thing.

shnorrer [Yidd] (shnor-ruh) Beggar.

schön [Ger] Beautiful; nice. *Schönheitsfarm* – health farm.

Schrecklichkeit [Ger] The deliberate perpetration of atrocities to subjugate a population.

schtroumpfe [Flemish] Equivalent to English 'thingummy'. *Schtroumpfes* was the name given by their Belgian creator to the little blue creatures we know as Smurfs.

schuss [Ger] (shooss) In skiing, a straight fast downhill run.

schwarz [Ger] Black, but like the English term 'black market' it can also mean 'illegal': *schwarzarbeiten* – earning extra untaxed income; *schwarzsehen* – to have a TV receiver without a licence.

scientiae causa [Lat] To carry out difficult or painful experiments in the cause of science.

scippo [It] Bag-snatching – unfortunately a common occurrence in Italian cities. *Scippatore* – bag-snatcher.

scudetto [It] *Lo Scudetto* – Italian First Division Soccer Championship for the tricolour shield. One of the top *Serie A* teams is AC Milan whose *tifosi* (supporters) fill Milan's San Siro stadium.

sculpsit [Lat] He/she sculpted it.

séance d'essais [Fr] A preliminary run by racing cars
before a race to familiarise drivers with the course.

se battre contre des moulins [Fr] To tilt at windmills.

secrétaire [Fr] An enclosed writing desk with a drop
writing table, drawers and pigeon-holes.

securus judicat orbis terrarum [Lat] The judgement of
the whole world cannot be wrong.

s'emmerder [Fr] Colloquial: to be bored.

semper fidelis [Lat] (sem-per fih-DAY-lis) Always faithful.
The motto of the United States Marine Corps.

semper in excretia sumus, solim profundum variat
[Lat] We are always in the shit, only the depth varies.

SEMPER IN EXCRETIA SUMUS

Senhor; Senhora; Senhorita [Port] Portuguese form of address for a man, married woman and unmarried woman respectively.

Señor; Señora; Señorita [Sp] The Spanish addresses for a man, married woman and unmarried woman respectively.

sensu abscaeno [Lat] To take the obscene meaning of a word or statement.

Serenissima, La [It] Colloquial for the Republic of Venice.

sérieux [Fr] Serious; sincere; earnest.

se soûler la gueule [Fr] Vulgar for 'to get drunk'.

sesquipedalia verba [Lat] Horace's pun 'Words of a foot and a half'; extremely long words.

seul [Fr] Alone; single. *Tout seul* – by oneself; *un homme seul* – a lonely man; *seul à seul* – tête-à-tête.

sgian-dhu [Gael] (skee-uhn doo) The dirk or knife carried in a Scottish Highlander's sock.

shaay [Arab] Tea.

shabash! [Hindi] Well done! Excellent!

shabat [Heb] The Sabbath.

shadchan [Yidd] A Jewish matchmaker or marriage broker.

shalom [Heb] (shah-LOM) Peace; hello. A common Jewish salutation.

shekel [Heb] Main Israeli unit of currency, divided into 100 *agorot* (singular *agora*).

shikker [Yidd] A drunk. *Shikkered* – to be drunk.

shiksa, shikseh [Yidd] An insulting term for a non-Jewish girl; a girl who is Jewish by birth but is non-practising.

shinkansen [Jap] Bullet train. The *hikari* is the express; the *kodama* is the high-speed stopping train.

shtik [Yidd] A routine unique to a performer; a special act.

shuk; suq [Arab] Open market-place. Usually spelt *souk*.

shul; schul [Yidd] A synagogue.

sic [Lat] Thus written; thus said. Used in brackets [*sic*] to indicate that a word, possibly misspelt, or a statement, possibly inaccurate, is being reproduced or quoted exactly.

sic semper tyrannis [Lat] Thus be the fate of tyrants. Uttered by Abraham Lincoln's assassin in 1865.

sic transit gloria mundi [Lat] Thus passes the glory of the world; worldly attainments are soon forgotten.

Sieg heil! [Ger] (zeek HYLE) Hail to victory: the infamous Nazi salute, accompanied by the raised arm.

si fractum non sit, noli id reficere [Lat] If it isn't broken, don't fix it.

Signor; Signora; Signorina [It] Italian forms of address for a man, married woman and unmarried woman respectively.

si jeunesse savait, si vieillesse pouvait [Fr] If youth but knew, if age but could.

s'il vous plaît [Fr] (sel-voo-play) If you please.

si parla italiano [It] Italian spoken here.

simpatico [It] Pleasant; likeable; nice. *Antipatico* – unpleasant; *simpaticone* – likeable person.

simplicissimus [Lat] A simple-minded man who, despite being exploited by others, is philosophical about his situation.

simpliste [Fr] Simplistic; too simple to be credible.

sine die [Lat] (see-nay dee-ay) Without a day or date being fixed.

sine qua non [Lat] (see-nay kwah non) An essential requirement or condition.

Sinn Féin [Ir] (shin-fayn) Literally, we ourselves. Irish republican movement founded in 1905; the political arm of the Irish Republican Army (IRA).

sirocco [It] (sih-ROH-koh) The wind that blows from the Sahara, north to Italy: warm, oppressive and sandy.

sit venia verbis [Lat] Pardon my words.

si vis pacem, para bellum [Lat] If you desire peace, prepare for war.

skal, skoal [Swed] Cheers! Good health!

sláinte [Gael] Good health!

smorgasbord [Swed] Traditional spread of food from salt fish, meats and salads through to hot dishes and cheese from which diners help themselves.

snobisme [Fr] Snobbery.

Sociedad Anónima; SA [Sp] Equivalent to the English Limited Company.

Société Anonyme; SA [Fr] French equivalent of the English Limited Company.

Société Nationale des Chemins de Fer; SNCF [Fr] The French nationalised railway system.

soi-disant [Fr] So-called; self-styled.

soigné [Fr] (swahn-yay) Elegantly groomed.

soirée [Fr] (swah-ray) An evening gathering where guests talk and listen or dance to music.

---

soixante-neuf

[Fr] (swas-ah(n)t-nuhrf) This little number is known to most schoolchildren well before their first French lessons. Or even history lessons:

Old Louis Quatorze was hot stuff.
He tired of that game, Blind Man's Buff,
    Up-ended his mistress,
    Kissed hers while she kissed his,
And thus taught the world *soixante-neuf.*

---

soldi [It] Money. ***Senza un soldo –*** broke of sans le sou.

son et lumière [Fr] (sohn ay loom-yair) Literally, sound and light. An evening entertainment staged outside a

historic building, with words, music and lighting effects
to illustrate its history.

sortes Biblicae [Lat] (sor-tez BIB-lee-kye) ('Biblical lots')
Prophesying by opening the Bible at any page and
selecting the passage the eye first sees; this passage is
prophetic. The same is done with the works of Virgil
and Homer.

sotto voce [It] (sot-toh VOH-chay) In an undertone.

sottogoverno [It] Italian political patronage whereby the
relatives of successful candidates and supporters of
victorious parties share government posts, jobs,
contracts and cash.

souk [Arab] See ***shuk***.

soupçon [Fr] (soop-soh(n)) A tiny amount; a dash.

soutane [Fr] (soo-tahn) Roman Catholic priest's cassock.

souteneur [Fr] A pimp or procurer.

spalpeen [Ir] Itinerant worker; layabout; rascal.

A Spanish conundrum

Knowing no English, a young Spanish woman entered a
London men's clothing store, Since the staff knew no
Spanish, she had great difficulty making herself
understood. However, in a flash of inspiration, one of the
salesmen began pointing to the various articles of clothing.
After several minutes he appeared to have hit on the
desired item. '*¡Eso sí que es!*' the young woman exclaimed,
using a Spanish expression that means 'That's it!'

The salesman, who was still under the impression that
she knew no English, was not amused by the time-wasting.
'Why didn't you spell it out for me at the start?' He asked.

What was the item of clothing the woman wanted?

(Answer on page 170)

Spätzündung [Ger] Literally, retarded ignition. ***Er hat
Spätzündung –*** he's slow on the uptake.

spécialité de la maison [Fr] The chef's special dish at a particular restaurant.

sperat infestis, metuit secundis [Lat] He hopes in adversity, fears in prosperity.

splendide mendax [Lat] Telling a lie for a good cause.

splitterfasernackt [Ger] Absolutely naked; starkers.

sprezzatura [It] The bravura or effortless technique of a great artist.

spurlos versunken [Ger] Sunk or vanished without trace.

Stabat Mater [Lat] Literally, the mother was standing. A Latin devotional poem that begins with these words.

Stammplatz [Ger] A favourite place.

stamppot [Dut] Traditional potato and vegetable hash, usually served with bacon and sausages.

Stasi [Ger] Abbreviation of *Staatssicherheitspolitzei,* East German Secret Police.

status quo [Lat] Existing or prevailing state of affairs.

stet [Lat] Let it stand. Used to say that an alteration marked on a printed proof should be ignored.

stet fortuna domus [Lat] May the fortunes of the house endure.

Stiefel [Ger] The peculiar large boot- or foot-shaped glass tankard filled with beer and passed from drinker to drinker at parties. The idea is to drink without the beer gurgling or surging out over the drinker.

stoep [Dut] (stoohp) The front verandah of a house.

Storbritannien [Swed] Great Britain.

Stundenhotel [Ger] At first sight a hostel for students but in fact a disorderly house or brothel.

Sturm und Drang [Ger] (shtoorm oont drahng) Literally, storm and stress. Originally an overheated German literary style; now an expression for tumult and extravagant passion.

style champêtre [Fr] In painting, idyllic pastoral scenes.

sua cuique sunt vitia [Lat] Every man has his vices.

sub judice [Lat] (sub DZHOO-dih-say) Under judicial consideration; as yet undecided by a court.

sub rosa [Lat] In secret; in strict confidence.

suburbio [Sp] In Latin American countries, the run-down shanty areas on the outskirts of cities.

succès de scandale [Fr] (sook-say duh skah(n)-dahl) Success of a play or book due to its scandalous nature.

succès d'estime [Fr] (sook-say deh-steem) Success of a play or book due to critical, rather than public, acclaim.

succès fou [Fr] (sook-say foo) A mad, wild, brilliant success.

suggestio falsi [Lat] Misrepresentation without actually lying.

sui generis [Lat] Of its own kind; unique.

summa cum laude [Lat] (sum-uh kum LOW-day) With the highest distinction; with the utmost praise.

summum bonum [Lat] The greatest good.

sumo [Jap] Japanese style of wrestling in which heavyweight opponents try to shove each other out of a ring.

Sunna [Arab] The body of Islamic law that orthodox Muslims accept as based on the words and acts of Muhammad.

supercherie [Fr] A hoax or fraud.

supermarché [Fr] Supermarket. A really large supermarket is called **un hypermarché**.

suppressio veri [Lat] Suppression of the truth; concealment of the facts.

supra vires [Lat] Beyond a person's powers.

Sûreté [Fr] (syoo-tay) French police criminal investigation department. **Sûreté Générale** – French equivalent of Britain's Scotland Yard.

sushi [Jap] Raw fish dishes; often small parcels of boiled rice wrapped in seaweed and topped with raw fish or vegetables.

suum cuique [Lat] To each his own.

Sverige [Swed] Sweden. *Svensk* – Swedish; *Svenska* –
Swedish language.

Systemzwang [Ger] A compulsion for system and order.

szálloda [Hun] Hotel. Smaller establishments, similar to
bed-and-breakfasts, are *panzió* and *fogadó*. Chalet-type
hotels for group accommodation are called *túristaszálló*.

T

tableau vivant [Fr] (tab-loh vih-vah(n)) A scene or painting represented by a posed group of still, silent people.

table d'hôte [Fr] (tab-luh doht) Fixed price restaurant menu with minimal choice.

tabula rasa [Lat] Literally, scraped tablet. A fresh surface ready to receive a new impression; a fresh mind open to receive information; an opportunity for a fresh start.

taedium vitae [Lat] Weariness of life.

Tageblätter [Ger] Newspapers.

tai chi chuan [Ch] Variety of Chinese unarmed combat; also used as a form of slow-moving callisthenic exercise.

taille [Fr] Clothes size. For shoes, socks, tights and gloves, size is expressed by *la pointure*.

Take Note: a Latin phrase quiz

Here's a little quiz to see if you have a living command of this 'dead' language. First, try to fill in the blanks in the following well-known Latin phrases, then have a go at deciphering Latin versions of some rather more familiar English originals.

1. **by itself**   *per —*
2. **among other things**   *—ter al—*

3. **note well**   *no— b—e*

4. *maxime fabulosum*   ————— **fabulous**

5. *emptrix nata sum*   **born to** ——

6. *libens, volens, potens*   **ready,** ——, ——

7. *dux coquorum et*   —— **cook and bottle** ——
      lavator amphorum

(Answers on page 170)

---

tamal; tamales [Sp] Hash of maize and meat wrapped in a leaf.

Tannenbaum [Ger] Christmas tree; pine tree.

tant mieux [Fr] (tah(n) myur) So much the better.

tant pis [Fr] (tah(n) pee) So much the worse.

Taoiseach [Ir] (TEE-sh uhle) Prime Minister of the Irish Republic.

tapas [Sp] Snacks served with drinks; also called *aperitivos*.

tapis [Fr] (tah-pee) A rug. *Un tapis de bain* – bathmat.

taramasalata [Gk] *Pâté* of cod's roe.

Tartufferie [Fr] Hypocrisy. Of which Molière's insincerely pious character **Tartuffe** was guilty.

tashinamu [Jap] Devotion to a cause with little likelihood of recognition or success.

taverna [Gk] A Greek restaurant where wine is served.

Taxe à Valeur Ajoutée; TVA [Fr] VAT or Value Added Tax.

tchin tchin [Fr] Cheers!

tchotchke [Yidd] A trinket or knicknack.

Te Deum [Lat] Thee, God, we praise. Hymn of praise and for giving thanks.

teishok [Jap] A fairly standard set meal of rice, soup, pickles and a selected dish. *Tonkats teishok* – set meal with pork as the main dish.

tel père, tel fils [Fr] Like father, like son.

témoignage [Fr] Factual, unprejudiced testimony.

tempora mutantur et nos mutamur in illis [Lat] Times change and we change with them.

tempura [Jap] Crispy deep-fried seafood and vegetables.

tempus fugit [Lat] Time flies.

tendresse [Fr] Affection; fondness; tenderness.

tenue de ville [Fr] Literally, town clothes; a man's lounge suit. *Tenue de soirée* is formal or evening dress.

tep-panyaki [Jap] Beef and vegetables grilled at the table.

terminus vitae [Lat] Death; end of life.

terra firma [Lat] Firm ground; solid earth; a land mass.

terra incognita [Lat] (teh-ruh in-KOG-nih-tuh) Unknown or unexplored regions.

tête-à-tête [Fr] (teht-ah-teht) A private conversation between two people.

Thai

Visitors to a temple in Bangkok are confronted with a sign which reads, 'It is forbidden to enter a woman'. Then, in smaller letters: 'Even a foreigner if dressed as a man'.

Thailand offers its millions of tourist visitors not only exotic food but also food for thought. For what would a diner make of 'Good Woman pullit' on the menu of a Bangkok restaurant? Or of a novelty doll sold by souvenir shops 'which laughs while you throw up'?

tibi seris, tibi metis [Lat] As ye sow, so shall ye reap.

tic douloureux [Fr] A neuralgic affliction characterized by twitching facial muscles.

tiens! [Fr] Really! You don't say! Well, well!

timbres-poste [Fr] Postage stamps.

timeo Danaos et dona ferentes [Lat] I fear the Greeks even when they bear gifts.

timor addidit alas [Lat] Fear gave him wings (Virgil).

tirez le rideau, la farce est jouée [Fr] Bring down the curtain, the farce is over, last words of Rabelais.

todo cae en el dedo malo [Sp] Everything falls on the injured finger.

tokaji [Hun] (toh-KAY) Hungarian wine made from the furmint grape. The famous sweet wines are *Aszu* and *Aszu Eszencia*.

tonto [Sp] Stupid; silly. *Una tontería* – a stupid thing.

topi; topee [Hindi] Sun hat; pith helmet.

Torah [Heb] The scroll on which Jewish law is written.

tortilla [Sp] (tor-TEE-yuh) Maize-flour pancake or omelette. Beware: *una tortillera* – vulgar in Spanish for lesbian.

Toto [Ger] *Länder* or state-controlled football pools in Germany.

totocalcio [It] Italian football pools. *La schedina* – pools coupon, on which punters have to enter their predictions. *Fare un tredici* – a win: all thirteen predictions correct.

toujours [Fr] (too-zhoor) Always; for ever.

toujours la politesse [Fr] It's always wise to be polite.

tour de force [Fr] (toor duh fors) A brilliant accomplishment.

Toussaint, La [Fr] All Saints' Day, November 1, which is followed on November 2 by *Le Jour des Morts* – All Souls' Day, when wreaths are placed on graves.

tout à vous [Fr] Yours truly.

tout comprendre c'est tout pardonner [Fr] To understand everything is to forgive everything.

tout court [Fr] Briefly; with nothing added; simply.

tout de suite [Fr] At once; immediately.

tout ensemble [Fr] (toot ah(n)-SAH(N)-buhl) All things considered; the total impression; general effect.

tout le monde [Fr] Everybody; the whole world.

tout ou rien [Fr] All or nothing.

tout passe, tout casse [Fr] Nothing lasts for ever.

traducteur [Fr] Translator. *Traduction* – translation.

traduttori traditori [It] Translators are traitors; true translation is impossible.

tranche de vie [Fr] 'Slice of life'.

trappistenbier [Dut] Beer originally brewed by Trappist monks.

trattoria [It] Restaurant or *ristorante*.

travailler [Fr] To work. *Un travailleur* – labourer; worker.

tredicesima [It] Thirteenth. *Tredicesima mensilità* or *la tredicesima* – the thirteenth or extra month's pay received prior to Christmas.

Treppenwitz [Ger] The clever riposte you think of – too late! See also **espirito de l'escalier**.

tricolore [Fr] (tree-KOL-ohr) Three-coloured. *Le drapeau tricolore* – the French flag, of *bleu, blanc et rouge*.

tricoteuse [Fr] One of the three women who knitted while watching the executions during the French Revolution.

Trinkgeld [Ger] In Germany, a tip; gratuity.

tristesse [Fr] Sadness; melancholy; gloom; depression.

troika [Rus] (troy-kuh) A carriage or sled pulled by three horses; a controlling body consisting of three people or groups sharing power.

trompe-l'œil [Fr] (tro(m)p luh-yuh) A painting that conveys the illusion of reality.

trop de cuisiniers gâtent la sauce [Fr] Too many cooks spoil the sauce.

trouvaille [Fr] (troo-vayuh) A lucky find; a windfall. *Trouver l'oiseau* – to find the rare bird; *trouver la perle* – to find a pearl.

truite [Fr] (trweet) Trout. *Truite saumonée* – salmon trout.

tsunami [Jap] Huge destructive wave caused by submarine earthquakes or volcanic eruptions.

tuan [Malay] Sir. Polite form of address by Malays.

tulp; tulpen [Dut] Tulips.

tu quoque [Lat] You too. Used by someone being accused
   of something to accuse the accuser in turn.

turista [Sp] A not altogether sympathetic name for
   travellers' diarrhoea in Central America.

TUTTE LE STRADE CONDUCONO A ROMA

Turkish delights

Not to be outdone, Turkey is yet another country to prove that *traduttore traditore* (q.v.). An Istanbul guide book sets the scene: 'The circumciser edifications make a fin stroll for all with a somptuous anfraction. Here old person can sit in the calme and yong lovers rumble under some dank and booming tress.' After the stroll you may retire to your hotel ('ALL ROOMS WITH FLYING WATER') or engage a local menu, featuring 'Girled Chaps, Cold tart of this House, Savages in Earthwore, Bowels in Spit, Trousers Stewed and Foul Salad'.

---

tutte le strade conducono a Roma [It] All roads lead to Rome.

tutti-frutti [It] (too-tih froo-tih) Fruit ice-cream.

tzatziki [Gk] Dip made from cucumber, yoghurt, garlic and oil.

Tziyonut [Heb] Zionism *Tziyoni* – a Zionist.

U

Übermensch [Ger] Superior man; a superman. From Nietzsche's *Also Sprach Zarathustra*.

ubi jus, ibi remedium [Lat] Where there is a right there is a remedy.

ubi lapsus? quid feci? [Lat] Where did I go wrong? What have I done?

ubi sunt qui ante nos fuerunt? [Lat] Where are those who have gone before us?

Übung macht den Meister [Ger] Practice makes the master.

ultima Thule [Lat] (UHL-tih-muh TOO-lih) The furthest limit; some faraway, unknown region.

ultra vires [Lat] (uhl-truh VEE-rays) Beyond the legal powers of a person or organization.

Um ein Haar [Ger] A close shave.

Umschwung [Ger] A sudden change of opinion or direction.

unberufen toi toi toi [Ger] An expression equivalent to the English 'touch wood' or 'knock on wood'.

uno ictu [Lat] At one blow.

uno saltu [Lat] With one bound; in a single leap.

un propos sale [Fr] A coarse remark.

Unterhosen [Ger] Underpants. *Schlüpfer* – undershorts. *Slip* – men's briefs and ladies' knickers; *die*

Unaussprechenlichen – the unmentionables.

unter vier Augen [Ger] Literally, under four eyes. Between two people only; between us; in confidence.

uovo [It] Egg. *Un uovo sodo* – a hard-boiled egg; *uova strapazzate* – scrambled eggs.

urbi et orbi [Lat] To the city and the world: the formal introduction for papal proclamations and blessings.

usus est tyrannus [Lat] Fashion or custom is a tyrant.

uyezd [Rus] In Russia, a district or county.

V

vade mecum [Lat] Literally, go with me. A guidebook or handbook to carry around.

vade retro, Satana! [Lat] Get thee behind me, Satan!

va fan culo [It] Extremely vulgar but all too common Italian expression meaning, roughly, 'Up your arse'.

vanitas vanitatum, omnia vanitas [Lat] Vanity of vanities, all is vanity.

vase de nuit [Fr] Chamber-pot. See *bourdalou*.

vashe zdarov'ye [Rus] Cheers! Used as a toast.

vero? [Lat] Really? You think so?

velatorio [Sp] Spanish wake – the twenty-four hours preceding a funeral during which the corpse is on view in its coffin.

velouté [Fr] A white sauce made with roux and stock.

vendeuse [Fr] (vah(n)-derz) Female sales assistant.

veniente occurrite morbo [Lat] Meet an approaching sickness; prevention is better than cure.

veni, vidi, vici [Lat] I came, I saw, I conquered. Julius Caesar's remark after his victory over Pharnaces.

ventre à terre [Fr] (vah(n)-truh ah-tair) Literally, belly to the earth. At full gallop; at full speed.

verbatim et literatim [Lat] Word for word, and letter for letter.

verboten [Ger] Forbidden; not allowed.

verbum sapienti sat est; verb. sap. [Lat] A word is enough for the wise. The abbreviation is used as a notice to the reader to take the preceding matter seriously.

veritas nunquam perit [Lat] Truth never dies.

veritas omnia vincit [Lat] Truth conquers everything. Often written *vincit omnia veritas*.

Verlag [Ger] Publisher; publishing house.

vers de société [Fr] Witty, topical verse.

vers libre [Fr] Unrhymed free verse.

vexata quaestio [Lat] A disputed point; a vexed question.

via [Lat and It] By way of; road; street. *Per via aerea* – by air mail; *via mare* – by sea; *via terra* – by land.

Via Crucis [Lat] The Stations of the Cross; the fourteen episodes in the Passion of Christ.

via dolorosa [Lat] Literally, sorrowful road. A series of distressing experiences. *Via Dolorosa* – Christ's route to Calvary and his crucifixion.

via media [Lat] A middle course; mid-way between extremes.

vice anglais [Fr] See *le vice anglais*.

victor ludorum [Lat] Winner of the games; a sports champion.

vide [Lat] (vee-day) Refer to; see. Used to direct a reader elsewhere in a book, or to another reference.

videlicet; viz [Lat] Namely; in other words. The abbreviation is used to introduce an example or explanation.

vie amoureuse [Fr] An account of someone's love affairs.

vie manquée [Fr] An ill-spent, wasted or misdirected life.

vieux jeu [Fr] (vyu zhu) Old-fashioned; out of date.

vieux marcheur [Fr] A man, well past it, who still pursues women.

vingt-et-un [Fr] (va(n)-tay-ur(n)) Twenty-one; blackjack; pontoon.

vin ordinaire [Fr] Cheap table wine.

virgo intacta [Lat] A woman who, is still a virgin.

visagisme [Fr] Beauty care and make-up. *Visagiste* – a beauty expert; cosmetician.

via medicatrix naturae [Lat] Nature's cure; natural recovery from ailments without medicine. *Vis-à-vis* [Fr] (veez-ah-vee) In relation to; regarding; face to face with.

vita brevis, ars longa [Lat] Life is short, art is long.

viva voce [Lat] (vy-vuh VOH-cheh) By word of mouth; orally; an oral examination 'viva'.

vive la différence! [Fr] (veev lah dee-feh-rah(n)s) Long live the difference!: usually applied to the difference between the sexes.

vivir y vivamos [Sp] Live and let live.

voilà! [Fr] (vwah-lah) There! See! Presto!

vol-au-vent [Fr] (vol-oh-vah(n)) Small savoury pastry.

volo comparare nonnulla tegumembra [Lat] I wish to purchase some condoms.

volte-face [Fr] A reversal of a previous policy or opinion.

vox populi, vox Dei [Lat] The voice of the people is the voice of God; public opinion rules.

voyez! [Fr] Look! See!

Wahlverwandtschaft [Ger] An intuitive or natural affinity between two people.

wàiguoren [Ch] Foreigner.

Walpurgisnacht [Ger] Walpurgis Night. The eve of the feast day of St Walpurga (May 1); in German folklore the night of the witches' sabbath.

Weihnachten [Ger] Christmas. *Heiligabend* – Christmas Eve.

Weinstube [Ger] German inn, serving wine and beer.

Weltanschauung [Ger] A philosophy of life; a person's philosophical outlook.

Weltschmerz [Ger] Sadness at the ills of the world; sentimentally pessimistic view of the world.

Wénhuà Dàgéming [Ch] The Cultural Revolution.

Wenn die Katze fort ist, tanzen die Mäuse [Ger] When the cat's away, the mice will play.

Wer den Sieg behält, der hat Recht [Ger] The victor is always in the right.

Wer ein Kalb stiehlt, stiehlt eine Kuh [Ger] He who steals a calf, steals a cow.

Wider den Strom schwimmen ist schwer [Ger] It's harder to swim against the current; don't kick against the pricks.

Winespeak

Every week, it seems, a few thousand more people become regular wine drinkers. And why not? The choice of wine today is breathtaking; hundreds of varieties pour in from dozens of countries and thousands of regions and makers. But with the wine comes a culture of wine terminology, most of it expressed in various foreign languages. A full list of all the names and terms you'll find on wine labels would require an encyclopaedia, but here, meanwhile, are some of the more common among them.

Appellation d'Origine Contrôlée [Fr] (a-pe-LA-syo(n) Do-ree-zheen-ko(n)-TRO- lay)	French legal designation guaranteeing the wine's geographical origin and quality.
blanc de blancs [Fr] (bla(n) duh bla(n))	White wine made only from white grapes.
brut [Fr] (broot)	Dry, when applied to sparkling wine.
cave [Fr] (kahv)	Cellar.
cépage [Fr]	The wine grape variety.
cru [Fr]	Growth; applied to a vineyard and the wine it makes.
Denominación de Origen [Sp]	Spanish equivalent of the French AOC (see above).
Denominazione di Origine Controllata [It]	The Italian equivalent of the French AOC (see above).
en primeur [Fr]	Buying future wine, still in cask.

flor [Sp] Literally: flower. A flavour-imparting yeast which grows on casked wine, usually sherry.

garrafeira [Port] Portuguese selected, aged wine.

négociant [Fr] Merchant who buys wine from growers for blending, ageing, bottling and resale.

mis en bouteille au château [Fr] Bottled at the château.

Qualitätswein [Ger] German wine classification for quality wines.

récoltant [Fr] Wine grower.

Spätlese [Ger] (shpayt-lay-zuh) Wine from sweet late-harvested grapes.

Tafelwein [Ger] Table wine.

vinho verde [Port] Green or young wine.

vinho maduro [Port] Wine that has aged.

Vins Délimités de Qualité Supérieure; VDQS [Fr] Controlled French wine category not quite up to the AOC standard.

---

wunderbar [Ger] (voon-duh-bar) Wonderful.
Wunderkind [Ger] (voon-duh-kint) A child prodigy.
Wurst [Ger] Sausage. **Blutwurst** – black pudding;
    Bockwurst – pink sausage; **Schinkenwurst** – ham
    sausage; **Bratwurst** – fried **Bockwurst**.

X

Xianggang [Ch] Hong Kong.
Xizang [Ch] Tibet.

Y

yad rochetset yad [Heb] You help me, I help you.

Yahadut [Heb] Judaism.

yakitori [Jap] Skewered chicken cooked on a grill.

yarmulke; yarmulka [Yidd] Skull-cap worn by Orthodox Jewish males.

yashmak [Arab] Face-concealing veil worn by Muslim women.

yeftah allah [Arab] The words that accompany an offer – usually well under the vendor's price – that a buyer is willing to pay, without giving offence.

yehudi [Heb] Jewish.

yenta [Yidd] A crude, loud, female gossip.

Yerushalayim [Heb] Jerusalem.

Yiddish

Yiddish, a blend of mostly German and some Hebrew, migrated during the last century to America where, even today, it continues to colour American English. *Fancy-schmancy* is fifth generation *Yidglish* but true Yiddishisms still surface. If you're called a **schmendrik,** start worrying; it means you think you're fantastic and cool but actually you've got a big hole in your trousers and you haven't noticed. Even so, it is better than being a *bupkiss* – a nothing.

Apart from its colour, Yiddish has a questioning quality: the propensity to answer a question with a question. – Why do Yiddish speakers do this? – Why shouldn't they? The answer lies in Genesis 4:9 – '...the Lord said unto Cain, where is Abel thy brother?' And what does Cain say? 'Am I my brother's keeper?' A true Yiddisher.

Yinggélán [Ch] England. *Yingguó* – Britain.

Yom Kippur [Heb] Annual Jewish Day of Atonement religious holiday.

yoni [Sans] In Hinduism, the venerated female genitalia.

Z

zabaglione [It] (zab-ah-lee-OH-nee) Whipped dessert of egg yolks, sugar and Marsala wine.

zapateado [Sp] The fast footwork and stamping feet of Spanish dancing.

Zeitgeist [Ger] (tzeyt-guyst) The attitude of a period; the spirit of the time.

Zeitung [Ger] Newspaper; journal.

zhela yoo oodachee! [Rus] Good luck!

Zhongguo [Ch] China. **Zhongguo rénmín** – the Chinese people.

Zijincheng [Ch] The Forbidden City.

zinc [Fr] Colloquial for the counter in a bar or café. **Manger sur le zinc** – eating at the bar.

Zivilcourage [Ger] To have the courage of one's convictions and to express them without fear.

zizi [Fr] Childish slang for male genitalia especially of young child.

zuppa [It] soup. **Zuppa di verdura** – vegetable soup; **zuppa di pesce** – fish soup.

Zwieback [Ger] (zwee-bahk) Baked bread rusk.

Answers to Tweak your Greek

1. mETAllic
2. caRHOp
3. PHIlosophy
4. caPSIze
5. maCHInery
6. resTAUrant

Answer to Spanish conundrum

The young lady genuinely knew no English but – by the most amazing coincidence – the phrase she uttered, **Eso sí que es,** also spells out socks, S-O-C-K-S.

Answers to Take Note

1. per SE
2. INter alIA
3. noTA bENe
4. ABSOLUTELY fabulous
5. born to SHOP (strictly, I am a born shopper)
6. ready, WILLING, ABLE
7. HEAD cook and bottle WASHER

Thirteen-Phrase Survival Guide in Thirteen Languages

You suddenly, unexpectedly, find yourself in a strange country. You don't understand what the natives are saying and they can't understand you. You revert to primitive sign language, trying to explain who you are, that you (pointing to empty pockets) have no money, that you need help. But sign language isn't enough. You desperately need just a few words and phrases to ease the way to understanding

The following rough survival guide – just thirteen expressions – provides the most elementary key to getting out of such a hypothetical situation in thirteen countries.

But don't suddenly, unexpectedly, land yourself in China. The complexities of translating Pinyin and its four tones are, regrettably, beyond the ultra-simplified format of our little Survival Guide.

ENGLISH	FRENCH	GERMAN
Yes	*oui*	*ja*
No	*non*	*nein*
Please	*s'il vous plaît*	*bitte*
Thank you	*merci*	*danke*
No thanks	*non merci*	*nein danke*
Sorry	*pardon*	*verzeihung*
Can you help me?	*Est-ce que vous pouvez m'aider?*	*Können Sie mir bitte helfen?*
I don't understand	*Je ne comprends pas*	*Ich verstehe nicht*
I don't speak...	*Je ne parle pas français*	*Ich spreche wenig Deutsch*
Do you speak English?	*Est-ce que vous parlez anglais?*	*Sprechen Sie Englisch?*
Where is the toilet?	*Où sont les toilettes?*	*Wo ist die Toilette?*
Goodbye	*au revoir*	*auf Wiedersehen*
Get lost!	*va t'en!*	*gehen Sie weg!*

ENGLISH	PORTUGUESE	SWEDISH
Yes	sim	ja
No	não	nej
Please	por favor	yars god
Thank you	obrigado	tack
No, thanks	não obrigado	nej tack
Sorry	desculp	förlat
Can you help me?	pode-me ajudar?	kan du hjälpa mig?
I don't understand	não compreendo	Jag förstår inte
I don't speak...	eu não falo português	Jag talar inte Svenska
Do you speak English?	Fala inglês?	Talar du Engelska?
Where is the toilet?	Onde é a casa de banho?	Var är toalett?
Goodbye	adeus	adjö
Get lost!	Vá'se embora!	förs vinn!

ENGLISH	GREEK	HUNGARIAN
Yes	*ne*	*igen*
No	*ochi*	*nem*
Please	*parakalo*	*kérem*
Thank you	*efkharisto*	*köszönöm*
No, thanks	*ochi, efkharisto*	*köszönöm nem*
Sorry	*signomi*	*elnézést net*
Can you help me?	*na me voithisis?*	*kérhetem a segítségét?*
I don't understand	*Then katalaveno*	*Nem ertem*
I don't speak...	*Then milao Elinika*	*Nem beszélek Magyarul*
Do you speak English?	*Milate Aglika?*	*Beszél angolul?*
Where is the toilet?	*Poo ine i toualeta?*	*Hol van a árnyékszék?*
Goodbye	*andio*	*viszontlátásra*
Get lost!	*fiye!*	*hagyjou békén!*

ENGLISH	DUTCH	JAPANESE
Yes	*ja*	*hai*
No	*nee*	*iya*
Please	*alstublieft*	*doozo*
Thank you	*dank u*	*domo arigato*
No, thanks	*nee, dank u*	*kekko des arigato*
Sorry	*spijt mij boris*	*sumi-masen*
Can you help me?	*kunt u mij helpen?*	*choto sumi-masen?*
I don't understand	*Ik begrijp het niet*	*Wakarimasen*
I don't speak...	*Ik spreek geen Nederlands*	*Nihongo wa hanasemasen*
Do you speak English?	*Spreekt u Engels?*	*Eigo a hanashimass ka?*
Where is the toilet?	*Waar zijn de toiletten?*	*toiret wa doko dess ka?*
Goodbye	*tot ziens*	*auf Wiedersehen*
Get lost!	*ga weg!*	*atchi e it-to!*

ENGLISH	ARABIC	HEBREW
Yes	naam	ken
No	laa	lo
Please	min	bewakaschar
Thank you	fadlek shoukran laa	todah
No, thanks	shoukran aasef min	lo todah
Sorry	fadlek	slik-ha
Can you help me?	momken tosa-aadnih?	efshah la'azor li?
I don't understand	Ma-afham	ani lo mevin
I don't speak...	Ma aqdar atakalam Arabee	ani lo medaber
Do you speak English?	Hal tatakalam Engleezi?	Ata medaber Anglit?
Where is the toilet?	wa-yu at-towaalet?	Afyo hasheruh?
Goodbye	maa as-salaamah	shalom
Get lost!	emshee!	lekh mi-po!

ENGLISH	ITALIAN	SPANISH
Yes	*sì*	*sí*
No	*no*	*no*
Please	*per favore*	*por favor*
Thank you	*grazie*	*gracias*
No, thanks	*no, grazie*	*no, gracias*
Sorry	*scusi*	*perdón*
Can you help me?	*può aiutarmi?*	*¿me puede ayudar?*
I don't understand	*non capisco*	*no entiendo*
I don't speak...	*non parlo italiano*	*no hablo español*
Do you speak English?	*parla inglese?*	*¿habla inglés?*
Where is the toilet?	*Dov'èe la toilette?*	*¿dónde están los aseos?*
Goodbye	*arrivederci*	*adiós*
Get lost!	*se ne vada!*	*¡váyase!*

Collins Wordpower

English is the most widely used language in the world, yet it is also one of the easiest languages to be misunderstood in. The Collins Wordpower series is the ultimate in user-friendliness for all who have wished for an authoritative, comprehensive yet accessible range of guides through the maze of English usage. Designed for ease of use and illustrated by top cartoonists, these books will enrich your powers of communication – whether in speech, writing, comprehension or general knowledge – and they are fun to use!

PUNCTUATION
0 00 472373 2
How to handle the "nuts and bolts" of English prose £5.99

GOOD GRAMMAR
0 00 472374 0
How to break down the barriers between you and clear communication £5.99

SUPER SPELLER
0 00 472371 6
How to master the most difficult-to-spell words and names in the English language £5.99

GOOD WRITING
0 00 472381 3
How to write clear and grammatically correct English £5.99

VOCABULARY EXPANDER
0 00 472382 1
How to dramatically increase your word power £5.99

ABBREVIATIONS
0 00 472389 9
The complete guide to abbreviations and acronyms £5.99

FOREIGN PHRASES
0 00 472388 0
The most commonly used foreign words in the English language £5.99

WORD CHECK
0 00 472378 3
How to deal with difficult and confusable words £5.99